The Psychological Technique
of Martin Luther Thomas'
Radio Addresses

The Psychological Technique
of Martin Luther Thomas'
Radio Addresses

Theodor W. Adorno

Stanford University Press
Stanford, California 2000

The Psychological Technique of Martin Luther Thomas'
Radio Addresses was originally published by Suhrkamp
Verlag in *Gesammelte Schriften* 9.1 (*Soziologische*
Schriften II, Erste Hälfte), © Suhrkamp Verlag Frankfurt
am Main 1975.

Stanford University Press
Stanford, California

Printed in the United States of America

Library of Congress Cataloging-in-Publication Data

Adorno, Theodor W., 1903–1969
The psychological technique of Martin Thomas' radio
addresses / Theodor W. Adorno
    p.   cm.
Includes bibliographical references.
ISBN 0-8047-4002-X (cloth: alk. paper) — ISBN 0-8047-4003-8
(paper: alk. paper)
1. Thomas, Martin Luther—Psychology. 2. Radio in
religion—United States—Case studies. 3. Radio in
propaganda—United States—Case studies. 4. Christianity
and politics—United States—Case studies. 5. Fascism—
United States—Case studies. I. Title.

BV3785.T44 A36 2000
302.23'44—dc21   00-024888

∞ This book is printed on acid-free, recycled paper.

Original printing 2000

Contents

I. THE PERSONAL ELEMENT: SELF-CHARACTERIZATION
    OF THE AGITATOR   1

Introductory Remarks, 1; "Lone Wolf," 4; "Emotional
Release" Device, 6; "Persecuted Innocence" Device, 10;
"Indefatigability" Device, 13; "Messenger" Device, 15;
"A Great Little Man," 18; "Human Interest," 24; "Good
Old Time," 25

II. THOMAS' METHOD   28

Introductory Remarks, 28; "Movement" Trick, 31;
"Flight-of-Ideas" Technique, 32; "Listen to Your Leader,"
37; Excursus on *"fait accompli"* Technique, 42; "Unity"
Trick, 47; The "Democratic Cloak," 50; "If You Only
Knew," 53; "Dirty Linen" Device, 58; "Tingling Back-
bone" Device, 61; "Last Hour" Device, 64; "Black Hand"
(*Feme*) Device, 68; "Let Us Be Practical," 70

III. THE RELIGIOUS MEDIUM   75

Introductory Remarks, 75; "Speaking with Tongues" De-
vice, 78; "Decomposition" (*Zersetzung*) Device, 81;
"Sheep and Bucks" Device, 85; "Personal Experience"
Device, 87; "Anti-Institution" Trick, 91; "Anti-Pharisees"
Device, 95; Religious Trickery in Operation, 98; "Faith of
Our Fathers" Device, 100

IV. *IDEOLOGICAL BAIT*   104

Introductory Remarks, 104; Imagery of Communism,
105; "Communists and Bankers" Device, 108; Adminis-
tration- and President-Baiting, 113; "Pick Up Thy Bed
and Walk" Device, 117; "The Jews Are Coming," 120;
"Problem" Device, 123; Conclusion, 130

The Psychological Technique
of Martin Luther Thomas'
Radio Addresses

The Personal Element:
Self-Characterization of the Agitator

Introductory Remarks

The fascist leader characteristically indulges in loquacious statements about himself. In contrast, the liberal as well as the radical propagandist has developed a tendency to avoid any reference to his private existence for the sake of "objective" interests to which he appeals: the former in order to show his matter-of-factness and competence, the latter because his collectivistic attitude would be jeopardized if he should play up his own personality. Whereas this "impersonality" is well grounded within the objective conditions of an industrial society, it has definite weaknesses considering the orator's audience. The detachment from personal relationships involved in any objective discussion presupposes an intellectual freedom and strength which hardly exists within the masses today. Moreover, the "coldness" inherent in objective argumentation intensifies the feeling of despair, isolation, and loneliness under which virtually each individual today suffers – a feeling from which he longs to escape when listening to any kind of public oratory. This situation has been grasped by the fascists. Their talk is personal. Not only does it refer to the most immediate interests of his listeners, but also it encompasses the sphere of privacy of the speaker himself who seems to take his listeners into his confidence and to bridge the gap between person and person.

There are more specific reasons for the attitude, which, though often nourished by the vanity of the leader, is well calculated and forms, in spite of its apparent "subjectivism," part of a highly objective set of propagandistic devices. The more impersonal our order becomes, the more important personality becomes as an ideology. The more the individual is reduced to a mere cog, the more the idea of the uniqueness of the individual, his autonomy and importance, has to be stressed as a compensation for his actual weakness. Since this cannot be done with each of the listeners individually or only in a rather general and abstract manner, it is done vicariously by the leader. It can even be said that part of the secret of totalitarian leadership is that the leader presents the image of an autonomous personality actually denied his followers.

Furthermore, the self-advertising of a fascist leader is a kind of a confidence trick. Although he occasionally boasts and can bluff in decisive moments, he prefers, especially before having achieved power, to play down the theme of his irresistible strength. He dwells upon his "also being human," that is to say, being as weak as his prospective adherents. The idea of strength and authority is not sufficient in itself to explain the appeal of fascist leadership. It is rather the idea that the weak can become strong if they surrender their own private existence to the "movement," the "cause," the "crusade" or whatever it may be. By referring to himself in an ambivalent way as both human and superhuman, weak and strong, close and far, the fascist leader supplies a model for the very attitude that he intends to affirm in his listeners.

In addition, his confessions, actual or faked, serve to satisfy the listener's curiosity. This is a universal feature in present-day mass culture. It is catered to by the gossip columns of certain newspapers, the inside stories told to innumerable listeners over the radio, or the magazines that promise "true stories." The structure of this curiosity has not yet been fully explored. It is due partly to the widespread feeling that one has to be "informed" in order to keep up with the conversation, partly to the feeling that the other fellow's life is rich, exciting and colorful, compared with the drudgery of one's own life. Perhaps more fundamentally, it is a function of the attitude of snooping, deep-rooted in the unconscious psychological process which longs for the gratification of catching a glimpse of one's neighbor's private life – an attitude closely akin to fascism. The leader is shrewd enough to realize that it does not make much difference how this curiosity is satisfied. Revelations about briberies or thefts supposedly committed by the foe, or discussions of his wife's illness or his financial difficulties which may even be invented are equally effective. As a practical psychologist, he knows something about ambivalence in action, even if he denounces psychoanalysis as a Jewish racket. The libido of the listener is satisfied when he is treated as an insider; it is a secondary matter whether his curiosity is directed at positive or negative concepts. If a foe fails to pay his bills, the fact may serve as a means to denounce him as a cheat. If Martin Luther Thomas, as he actually did, states in public that he cannot pay his radio expenses, this very statement may win him new friends.

There is finally an "objective" reason for the fascist's lack of objectivity. It helps either to hide or to obscure his objective aims. In America where, unlike Germany, the idea of democracy has a great tradition and a strong emotional appeal, it would be highly impractical for any fascist leader to attack democracy itself, as the Nazi propagandists freely did. The American fascist is generally prepared to accept democracy as a cloak for his own ends. However, by plugging himself and by applying a technique of high-pressure publicity, he hopes to secure so much power as to build up a tremendous pressure group which may finally overthrow democracy in the name of democracy – the Huey Long prescription. Apart from that, it is a well known technique of fascist propaganda to promise vaguely everything to every group without bothering too much about conflicting group interests. When he speaks about himself, he accumulates confidence for his power of integration; on the other hand he must become so specific about his objective purposes that the self-contradictory features of his program do not become too blatant. Thus the personal touch is efficient camouflage.

Martin Luther Thomas is thoroughly acquainted with the Hitler technique through his affiliations with Deatheradge, Henry Allen, and Mrs. Fry. He knows everything about the manipulation of his own ego for propagandist purposes and has skillfully adapted the Hitlerian technique of revelation and confession to the American scene and to the emotional needs of the group to which he addresses himself – the middle-aged

and elderly, lower-middle-class people with a strong fundamentalist or sectarian religious background. The following
are some examples of the way in which he talks about himself.

"Lone wolf"

There is first of all the "lone wolf" trick. It is taken from the
arsenal of Hitler, who always used to boast about the seven
lonely and heroic party comrades who began the movement,
and about the fact that others controlled the press, the radio
– everything; and that he had nothing. Thomas slightly
modifies this by specifically insisting he has no politician's
money behind him. He uses innumerable times variations of
the statement: "I have no sponsors, and no politicians ever put
one dollar into this movement."[1] This modification results
from Thomas' playing upon the American distrust of the
professional politician who is supposed to profit privately by
making a racket of public matters. Since Thomas himself, like
his fellow agitators, shows all the characteristics of a political
racketeer, he is all the more anxious to shift the onus of such
an occupation upon those from whom he claims to be detached.
Fewer, he reasons, will believe him a racketeer, if he thus
violently attacks racketeering. It is incidentally one of the
most outstanding characteristics of fascist and anti-Semitic
propagandists that they blame their victims in an almost
compulsory way for exactly the things which they themselves
are doing or hope to do. Counterpropaganda should conse-
quently point out concretely that they are doing the self-same
things about which they profess to be furious. There is practically no category of fascist propaganda to which this rule
cannot be applied. It is this pattern through which the
mechanism of psychological "projection" makes itself felt
throughout fascist ideology.
Apart from playing up one's own courage and integrity in
order to win the confidence of those who feel that they are
underdogs and alone, there is a deeper calculation implied in

1 May 29, 1934.

the "lone wolf" device. It allays the universal and ever-increasing fear of manipulation. This fear grows out of sales resistance and terminates in the semi-conscious belief that no word uttered in public has either objective significance or represents even the speaker's private conviction. It is thought of as propaganda in the broadest sense, serving the interest of some strong agency paying for every public statement that is made. The reason for this attitude lies, of course, in the economic centralization and monopolization of the channels of communication. The claim that "no politician's money is behind me" amounts to the pretention that the statements one makes are spontaneous – not yet directed by monopolistic organization. However, that attitude towards manipulation and, therefore, the psychological function of this device must not be oversimplified. Under present social conditions, people are not only afraid of manipulation, but also, conversely, they long for it and for the guidance of those who they realize are strong and capable of protecting them. The hierarchical nature of our economic organization has increased the desire to be passively manipulated. Moreover, the borderline between "objective statements" and propagandistic devices begins to become more and more fluid. The more power is concentrated in the agencies and individuals who control the channels of communication, the more their propaganda amounts to "truth" insofar as it expresses true power relations. It is highly significant that in Germany the Goebbels office is called the *Ministerium für Volksaufklärung und Propaganda* (ministry of public enlightenment and propaganda) and thus in its very name identifies objective truth, about which one is supposed to be enlightened, with the propaganda words of the party. This ambiguity toward manipulation is to be taken into account by the propagandists who use the "lone wolf" device. They do not expect it to be taken quite seriously, and it probably never is. While they play upon public distrust of manipulation by the present powers within communications and party politics, they suggest with the "lone wolf" trick that in fact very much is behind them, namely the true powers that be, as opposed to the official title holders. In the present phase, stirring up hatred against monopolism is one of the means of promoting the final victory of totalitarianism. The listener who hears daily over a big radio station that the speaker is lonely and working on his own account, realizes that he is not backed by the openly known and established agencies of today but rather by the potential power of the integrated collectivity and the "secret kingdom to come" of which one becomes a citizen by submerging oneself in it as early as possible. Just the defamation of manipulation is the means of manipulation. People are skillfully made to believe that the initiative is with them and their model, the speaker. The more they are stripped of spontaneity, the more their supposed spontaneity is upheld as an ideology.

"Emotional release" device

The speaker's simulation of spontaneity and non-manip-ulated individuality is underscored by a particular pattern of behavior which he not only exhibits but also recommends. He is consciously and emphatically emotional as part of his technique. He reiterates on many occasions that he "almost cried" when he got a contribution of fifty cents from that poor old widow. Whereas his whole personal build-up is that of the leader, he conspicuously refrains from any attitude of "dig-nity." Just this abandonment of dignity is apparently one of the effective stimuli of fascist propaganda everywhere. Hitler himself was always prone to ostentatious, hysterical outbreaks, and one of his favorite phrases was "I should rather shoot myself than . . ." In Thomas' speeches the "emotional release" device is derived from his religious attitude, his evangelistic, revivalistic penchant, in contrast to official Presbyterianism.

You know I thank God that I am kind of turning loose of my heart the last three years. You know for a Presbyterian who has been reared in the suppression of the outward manifestation of the heart, you know it is a great thing. Listen, Presbyterians and Episcopalians, and all those schools of stoicism: turn loose of your heart! Oh, I know how hard it is. You kind of feel like I do. You are afraid of fanaticism.[2] There is a rightful place for the expression of love for God. You needn't be a fanatic. Remember what St. Augustine said one day: "If you let your heart loose, you will toddle off to God." Clap your hands just a little bit. Remember over yonder in the Old Testament, remember where it says that the trees have clapped their hands for joy. All nature praised the Creator! That wonderful flower as it blooms and nods in the sun, no human eye will ever see it. No animal will ever notice it. It is praising and smiling for its God. All of the earth is filled with the glory. The prophets cried the earth is filled with the glory of the Lord. My, it is wonderful to know God, isn't it? It is wonderful to know Christ.[3]

In such passages as this Thomas involuntarily reveals his true intentions. His own emotionalism serves only as a model for the behavior that he wishes his listeners to develop by imitation. He wants them to cry, to gesticulate, to give way to their feelings. They should not behave so well and be so civilized. Under the cloak of Christian ecstasy, there is the encouragement to paganism, to the orgiastic release of one's emotional drives, to regression towards inarticulate nature, which worked so successfully in Nazi propaganda. The ultimate aim of the "emotional release" device is the encouragement and endorsement of excess and violence. As soon as the barriers against crying and self-pity are broken down, one may express unchecked one's suppressed feelings of hatred and fury as well, and the collective religious wantonness of the Holy Rollers may be consummated by the pogrom. Moreover, the more the barriers of self-control within the listeners are broken down by the orator's encouragement, the more easily they are subjected to his will rather than to their own, and to following him blindly wherever he wants them to go.

It has often been pointed out that fascism feeds upon the lack of emotional gratification in an industrial society and that it grants to the people that irrational satisfaction which is denied them by today's social and economic setup. The "emotional release" device primarily corroborates this assumption. The concept ought to be qualified, however, in other respects in order to fit it with reality.

2 Hitler often spoke about his own "fanatical love for Germany."
3 July 9, 1935.

First, ideology and reality must not be confused. The irrational gratifications which fascism offers are themselves planned and handled in an utterly rational way. Such manipulation results in a kind of psycho-technics, borrowed from the modern factory and applied to the population as a whole. It is an extremely pragmatic irrationality, and it is highly characteristic that this irrationality is expressly advertised by Thomas as well as by the German agitators as if it were a kind of a pill which makes life more agreeable. It is important to bear this in mind since this rational aspect of fascist irrational propaganda (as well as, for example, the "escapist" presentations of modern mass culture) is so obvious that it must produce a certain resistance against the permanent insincerity, a resistance which could be used by counterpropaganda. The latter might point out the shrewd soberness behind the drunken words. Such an attack would place the fascists in an inescapable dilemma, for fascist propaganda cannot avoid this rationalism within the sphere of emotional release. The fascist agitator has to reckon with people as they are, sober and practical, and can induce them to irrational attitudes only if he makes them appear as "sensible" according to the psychological economy of their own lives.

Second, the manipulated irrational gratifications are spurious. Manipulation itself is intrinsically opposed to that "release" which it sets in motion. Moreover, fascist propaganda for its own purposes does not touch upon the roots of emotional frustration in our society but rather encourages emotionalism by words. There is no real pleasure or joy, but only the release of the feeling of one's own unhappiness and the achievement of a retrogressive gratification out of the submergence of the self into the community. In short, the emotional release presented by fascism is a mere substitute for the fulfillment of desires. The most drastic example is Father Divine's device of applying an enthusiastic "it's wonderful" to everything – and therewith to nothing. When Thomas dwells on the marvelous weather, the beautiful Southern Californian landscape and the blossoming flowers, his trick is not unlike that of the Negro evangelist, for the beautiful things that he praises and offers as objects of unchecked emotions have little to do with the social world of his listeners, and even less to do with his own objectives.[4] One may suspect that any reference to the emotional resources of nature is part of a scheme to distract the audience from actual problems.

Third, the switching on of emotionalism is not altogether a device superimposed upon the listeners. It presupposes a certain disposition within them, and so the shrewdness of a successful agitator actually consists in sensing dispositions which he can use as bait for his own purposes. A strong basis for the desire to escape the rigidity of psychological self-control must exist in the listeners themselves, and hence an adequate idea of this "basis" must be developed. It is in itself a result of the very same process of rationalization from which people want to get away. People want to "give in," to cease to be individuals in the traditional sense of a self-sustaining and self-controlled unity, because they must. Thomas' negative references to stoicism and to the self-control required by the established denominations are not accidental. This stoicism is part of the attitude of the independent individual of the liberal era of free competition. The strength to control oneself reflects the strength to compete with others and to determine economically and thus also psychologically one's own fate. Today, when this independence begins more and more to dwindle, self-control begins to disappear too. The social forces to which each individual is subject are so tremendous that he has to yield to them not only economically by becoming an employee (rather than remaining a self-sustaining social unit), but also psychologically under the social and cultural pressure put upon him, a pressure which he can bear only by making it his own cause. He must act in terms of adequate conformist behavior rather than in the terms of a unified, integrated personality. The individual becomes not only harder insofar

4 Some examples: "Our father, we thank you this afternoon for this wonderful day. We thank thee for this beautiful Southern land." (July 14, 1935) – "Good morning, everybody, everywhere. We are happy to be with you upon this beautiful day with the sunshine pouring out upon your yards." (July 3, 1935)

as he is taught to think more and more pragmatically. He also becomes softer insofar as his resistance to the impact of the social world as a whole and industrial technology in particular becomes weaker. The more he ceases to be an ego, a "self," the less he is capable and willing to fulfill the requirements of self-control. Hysteria is an extreme expression of a psychological configuration spreading rapidly over the whole of society. It is this particular disposition which is met by the "emotional release" device. Stoicism is derided because the individuals neither can nor will be stoical any longer, that is to say, because the final compensation for emotional self-control – an existence firmly established in itself and secure – no longer prevails. The effect of the emotional release device is not so much that it evinces the reactions to which it refers, but rather that it makes them socially acceptable and lifts an already tottering taboo so that people may have the feeling of doing the socially correct thing if they abandon their self-control. This mechanism of a "social affirmation" of attitudes which already operate within the subjects but which they still vaguely feel to be at variance with the rules that they were taught in their youth is an intrinsic element of all fascist and anti-Semitic propaganda.

"Persecuted innocence" device

The selection of the personal qualities the speaker directly or indirectly claims to possess gains significance only with reference to some which are conspicuously absent. He stresses, for example, his personal integrity and honesty, therewith falling in line with old patterns of election propaganda. He also hints at his qualifications as a leader. But he never refers to his particular equipment for doing the rather ill-defined job upon which he embarks. He points out neither his training, his political background, his erudition nor any specific personal features by which he may qualify as a political leader. Instead he is satisfied by vaguely referring to God's call. The configuration of self-advertising and vagueness about himself has a meaning of its own. Apart from possibly calculating upon the widespread aversion to the professional politician and perhaps to any kind of expertness, a feeling based upon the deep-rooted unconscious resistance to the prevailing division of labor, Thomas uses the vagueness of his image of himself to leave room for any kind of fantasy on the part of the audience. He presents himself as a kind of empty frame which can be filled out by the most contradictory conceptions on the part of his listeners. He may be imagined by them as a benevolent and humane clergyman, or as a reckless soldier, as a high-strung, emotional human being or as a shrewd man of practical life, as a keen observer who knows all dubious inside stories and as a pure soul who calls in the wilderness. Vagueness about his own personality is a means of integration concomitant with the vagueness of his political aims. Both serve to herd together most different types of listeners who are willing to follow him the more blindly, the less exactly they know who he is and what he stands for. A certain abstractness, interspersed with petty concrete references to daily life, is characteristic of the pattern of the fascist agitator.

There are, however, some few specific traits which occur again and again. First, the dwelling upon his own innocence. He is not merely an irreproachable and unselfish character, and it is just because of his higher moral qualities that he is subject to permanent persecution – to threats and conspiracies of his enemies. Thomas goes often so far as to say that he may be poisoned at any time or that his church (which, by the way, was his private property) may be burnt. "People will write all kinds of things. They write everything against me. They write that they are going to kill me."[5] Other West Coast fascist agitators, such as [George] A. Phelps, also imply the "persecuted innocence" device which was developed by the Nazis. The latter characteristically called their highly aggressive elite guard (from which the Gestapo members are selected) the SS, *Schutzstaffel*, that is to say, "protective Corps." The "persecuted innocence" device serves a double purpose. First, it has to interpret the danger to the leader as one to all and to rationalize aggressiveness under the guise of self-defence.

5 May 22, 1935.

"Listen Christians, do you remember what he said: if they
have persecuted me they will also persecute you."[6] The most
pronounced example of this trick is provided by Father
[Charles Edward] Coughlin's excuse for Hitlerism in all
its aspects by referring to it in terms of a "self-defense mechanism." It is borrowed from high politics. Ever since Caesar
attacked the half-savage Gauls with his highly trained army
and explained his war of conquest as a consequence of absolutely necessary protective measures, military aggression has
been termed defense. Fascism with its intrinsic affinity to all
imperialistic behavior patterns has, for the first time, adapted
this device to the purpose of home policy and even to the
building up of ideologies for individual actions. There
is, however, a deeper psychological implication in the mechanism. It is not expected that it will be taken completely seriously
but rather as a stimulus to violence itself. In this connection,
psychoanalysis has shown that the aggressive, sadistic tendencies to which Fascist propaganda appeals do not clearly
differentiate between the aggressor and the victim: psychologically, both notions are to a certain extent interchangeable,
since both date back to a developmental phase where the
distinction between subject and object, ego and outer world, is
not yet clearly established. This ambivalence is further evi-
denced by the large role of the concept of self-sacrifice in all
fascist propaganda. In the last analysis, such an interchange-
ability makes it possible to blame the prospective victim for
the very same crime one wants to commit oneself. By "projection" one unconsciously makes events appear real which exist
only in one's own imagination. The most blatant example of
this mechanism is, of course, the German Reichstag fire. In
Germany, the "persecuted innocence" device always was used
with a certain cynicism and was received as such. For example,
innumerable jokes of the type "Jew peddler bites Aryan
shepherd dog" were enjoyed. It is very likely that the same
device is applied on the American scene in a parallel way.

6 July 13, 1935.

"Indefatigability" device

While referring to his own persecuted honesty, unselfishness and devotion to the great cause, Thomas rarely forgets to hint at his indefatigability. He reads hundreds of letters a day; he spends his last bit of energy; his hair was turned gray too early because of his ceaseless efforts; he sacrifices, and works, incomparably more than his followers: "Let me repeat that my work is a labor of love. I am asking you only to sacrifice with me. I don't ask you to work as hard as I work."[7] Indefatigability, strangely enough, is also one of the main characteristics he ascribes to his foes. The Bolsheviks are never tired; they are at their subversive work day and night, undermining the structure of American society while the good folks are asleep. "Remember, the Communists never take a vacation. Remember, the devil has a revivial all of the time. You and I must work night and day simply because we have less than a half loaf."[8] The affinity of this device to the "Germany awaken" theme lies at hand. Its psychological implications are manifold and not altogether consistent.
There is, above all, the desire to "stir up," which may be regarded as the archetype of all aggressiveness. It is one of the innermost drives of fascism to perpetuate actually and ideologically the necessity of hard work, thus obtaining a justification for "discipline" and oppression. This attitude, grounded in socioeconomic tendencies, permeates the whole fascist setup into its last psychological ramifications. Under fascism, psychologically, no one is allowed to sleep: one of the favorite tortures applied by authoritarian governments to their victims is that their sleep is interrupted hourly until their nerves completely break down. The fascist hatred of sleep – in the broadest sense of leaving anything alone – is reflected by the fascist leader's emphasis upon his being indefatigable himself, therewith setting an example for his followers. Indefatigability is a psychological expression of totalitarianism. No rest should be given, unless everything is seized, grasped, organized. And

7 May 22, 1935.
8 May 31, 1935.

since this aim will never be reached, the ceaseless efforts of
every follower are needed.[9]

Yet, while indefatigability is stressed, the agitator does not
actually want to evince a fully "awake," conscious, lucid
attitude in his followers. To be sure, he wants them to be
active and to be ready to do things, but only under a kind of
spell. There is an element of truth in the reference to "mass
hypnotism" in fascism, though this reference often underrates
the highly "rational" element in fascist mass movements, the
followers' hope for material gain and an improvement of
their social status. However, so much may safely be said: It is
the activity of the hypnotized which is expected by fascist
propaganda rather than that of responsible and conscious
individuals. Thus, the insistence upon indefatigability works
as a kind of dope. Just because the follower is expected, in a
way, to fall asleep and to act while he is asleep, he is told innumerable times that he has to be awake and that he must not
sleep. The relationship between sleeping and indefatigability is
highly ambivalent and the agitators feed upon this ambivalence. He who is to sleep while he is told that he has to be
indefatigable and that he is indefatigable, may offer much less

9 It goes without saying that the praise of indefatigability is deeply rooted
throughout middle-class society. It plays a decisive role particularly in
Calvinism and Jansenism. Pascal went so far as to define Christianity in
terms of indefatigability: the agony of Christ lasts until the end of the
world, and no one should sleep any more. The more radical, ascetic Christian movements always emphasized this point, and it may obtain its
peculiar weight within Thomas' propaganda through this "revivalist"
background. The term revival itself implies hostility against anything that
rests quietly. What is new about the indefatigability device in fascism is
only that it has been made independent, a sort of fetish. The older bourgeois
had to be indefatigable in order to secure a chance of winning the pity of
the hidden God and of making a fortune for his family. The fascist is
taught to be indefatigable for the sake of indefatigability itself. Self-denial,
in this as in all other respects, is interpreted in terms of an end rather than a
means. It is regarded as the very same compensation which it forbids. This
transformation is one of the deepest psychological changes that have taken
place in our time. It would be essential for any counterpropaganda, which
really gets at the hub of the problems, to point out the irrational, fetishistic,
and absurd characteristics of all the "sacrifices" demanded by fascist propaganda.

resistance to the will of his leader than he otherwise would. He is made to believe himself vaccinated against the very contagion that threatens him.[10]

"Messenger" device

There is one last very specific characteristic Thomas applies to himself – a characteristic which is especially noteworthy since it overtly contradicts the image of the leader, whereas in a deeper sense it is likely to be intrinsically connected with the fascist leader type. It is the idea that the speaker himself is not the savior, but only his messenger. In Thomas' speeches the "messenger" device is borrowed from the theological armory, namely, from the role of St. John the Baptist.

John had sense enough to know that he could not take this other place. John recognized that he had his own gift, but it was not to step into the light of the cross of Jesus. Here is a tremendous truth that you and I need to recognize and to obey. If this message that I am giving today glorifies Martin Luther Thomas or any other human being, it is bound to fail, but if this message of the great Christian American Crusade lifts up the Son of God, this movement is bound to succeed. . . . I do not know what your talents in life may be. It may

10 The question how the "hypnotic" and the "rational" element work together in fascist propaganda may be answered at least tentatively. Above all, fascist propaganda cannot be *entirely* rational, for objective reasons. Fascism aims at the repressive maintenance of an antagonistic society – an aim which is intrinsically irrational. It is rational only with reference to the interest of single groups or individuals. The discrepancy between such interests and the irrationality of the whole makes itself keenly felt. One may well assume that the hidden awareness of the irrationality of the final goals of the "movement" produces some sort of bad conscience within each individual fascist. Here the hypnotic element comes into play. It helps to overcome that bad conscience. The fascist stops thinking, not because he is stupid and does not see his own interest, but because he does not want to acknowledge the conflict between his particular interest and that of the whole. He gives up his reasoning because it is "rationally" inconvenient to him. There is an element of spitefulness involved in his "belief." He has to switch it on himself, again and again, in order not to lose his spurious faith. Fascist hypnotism may be characterized as being essentially self-hypnotism.

be that you are simply to be a messenger. Now the finest place in the world is to be a messenger. Now, I am a messenger of God to the world; so are you."[11]

We are not concerned at this point with the well calculated confusion of worldly and spiritual matters – the cross of Jesus and the Christian American Crusade. We are merely concerned with the idea of the messenger and Thomas' stressing that he is a prophet rather than a fulfiller of the hopes which he elicits. This may appear to be an accidental feature of this particular agitator which has little to do with the essence of fascist propaganda where the leader is primarily expected to play himself up. But it should not be overlooked that Hitler, during the earlier days of Nazism, employed the messenger device too, by calling himself merely the drummer ("*Ich bin nur der Trommler*"). The obvious reason for this device is, of course, that many fascist leaders were originally propagandists rather than actual politicians – which in itself is a significant feature of our present society where the borderline between advertizing and reality has become so fluent. However, there is a deeper psychological issue involved. Some light may be thrown upon it by an occasional reference of Thomas to his father: "My father was a very brainy man. Unfortunately his son didn't inherit any of his brains."[12] This propagandistic, ironic humility is a thin veil for the speaker's antagonism to his father (an antagonism which becomes apparent at other passages as well, particularly when Thomas contrasts his religious fervor to his father's supposed "agnosticism"). Hitler's *Mein Kampf* leaves no doubt that he, too, went through severe psychological and practical conflicts with his father. It is hardly too daring a venture to interpret the drummer or messenger device as an expression of the speaker's desire to present himself as the image of the *son*, of him who is not yet "the man" himself.[13] Incidentally, the emphasis

11 May 23, 1935.
12 May 29, 1935.
13 This idea, which has been developed by the Institute of Social Research for many years, has been printed out independently, and somewhat differently, in Erik Homburger Erikson's study, "Hitler's Imagery and German

upon the concept of the Son as contrasted to that of God the Father is one of the central points of Thomas' theological twists. The Agitator who wishes his followers to identify themselves with him and to imitate him presents himself not only as their superior, as the strong man, but simultaneously as just the opposite. He is as weak as they are; he is the one who needs redemption rather than he who redeems, in short, he is a son subject to paternal authority, dependent on and at the service of something bigger than himself.[14] This greater entity is, however, no longer the father. It is vague and utterly undefined, but all the stimuli point to its being the collectivity of all the "sons" gathered around the fascist organization – a collectivity the power of which is supposed to give psycho-logical compensation for the weakness of each component individual. The image of the fascist dictator is no longer a paternalistic one. This fact reflects the decline of the family as a self-sustaining, independent, economic unit in the present phase of social development. As the father ceases to be the guarantor of the life of his family, so he ceases to represent psychologically a superior social agency. The image of Stalin still has something orientally patriarchal, in Mussolini patri-

Youth": "Psychologists overdo Hitler's father attributes. Hitler is the adolescent who never even aspired to become a father in any connotation, nor, for that matter, a kaiser, or a president. He does not repeat Napo-leon's error. He is the Führer: *a glorified older brother*, who replaces the father, taking over all his prerogatives, without over-identifying with him: he calls his father 'old while still a child' and reserves for himself the new position of the one who remains young in possession of supreme power. He is the unbroken adolescent who has chosen a career apart from civilian happiness and 'peace'; a gang leader who keeps 'the boys' together by demanding their admiration, by creating terror, and by shrewdly involving them in crimes from which there is no way back. And he is a ruthless ex-ploiter of parental failure." (*Psychiatry* V, 4 [November, 1942], pp. 480-481.)

14 This motive is, strangely enough, to be found at the end of Wagner's *Parsifal* which, as a whole, is a sort of anti-Semitic cryptogram. The last words of the opera are "*Erlösung dem Erlöser.*" Paternalistic authority as represented by Titurel is shown as being utterly powerless throughout the opera: Titurel has abdicated for the sake of his son Amfortas and dies for the latter's sin.

archal features are faintly hinted at, but they are totally
absent in the bachelor Hitler and his collective image. Hitler
himself represents much more the rebellious, neurotically weak
son who succeeds just by his neurotic weakness which enables
him to submerge completely with his equals in the movement.
The fascist leader is supposed to gain control by "giving himself up" and surrendering himself to the collectivity. It is
from the latter that he derives his authority and for which he
stands in all his symbolic utterances – hence, the tendency to
stress that he is not the savior himself but merely his messenger
or representative. Thomas, who mainly appeals to middle-aged
people of a strong Christian background, is, as a whole, more
patriarchal than the more streamlined fascist leader types.
This, by the way, does not make him less dangerous, since
his specific qualifications allow him to affect groups which
otherwise might be very difficult to reach by propaganda.[15]
Nevertheless, he cannot entirely dispense with the "son" aspect
of Fascism which makes itself felt in his assurance of humility,
his devotion to something greater than himself, and his being
merely a forerunner of what is to come. The real psychological
trick of fascism consists in the fact that the forerunner is
transformed by certain unconscious mechanisms into him
whom he is supposed to announce.

"A great little man"

Apart from its far-reaching unconscious implications, the
messenger device belongs to a much more general structure of
fascist propaganda. It points into a constellation which is
characteristic for the whole relationship between the speaker

15 It may be noted that a kind of psychological "division of labor" also
took place among the German fascist leaders. Hitler himself stressed, in his
New Year's message of 1934, the diversity of Nazi leader types. Apart
from extremely non-paternalistic and even homosexual types such as Hitler,
Röhm, Schirach and Goebbels, there are more patriarchal ones, such as the
"civil service" man Frick. However, the appeal of the latter group seems to
have decreased considerably since the Nazis came into power.

and his audience. Representing the psychological "integration" of his audience as a totality, he is both weak and strong: weak insofar as each member of the crowd is conceived as being capable of identifying himself with the leader who, therefore, must not be too superior to the follower; strong insofar as he represents the powerful collectivity which is achieved through the unification of those whom he addresses. The image that he presents of himself is that of the "great little man" with a touch of the incognito, of he who walks unrecognized in the same paths as other folks, but who finally is to be revealed as the savior. He calls for both intimate identification and adulating aloofness; hence, his picture is purposely self-contradictory. He reckons with short memories and relies rather on the divergent unconscious dispositions to which he appeals at different times, than on consistent rational convictions.

There are two specific evidences of the great little man device. The first is Thomas' attitude towards money, or the way in which he speaks of his financial worries. As far as is known, Thomas had no powerful financial backing, though the role he played in the Merriam-Sinclair campaign (as well as some other factors) suggests that he was not quite without any important financial sponsors. Even if it is true, however, that he had to rely mainly on the small contributions that he received from his radio listeners, the way in which he discusses money with them is rather unusual. No consideration of dignity inhibits him from asking for money again and again; no religious scruples are in his way to prevent him from mixing up religious and financial issues in a fashion which one would expect to be revolting to any religious person. All his speeches are interspersed with whining and pointedly shameless appeals for funds; one may say that he plays the beggar. This habit was common in the period of the rise of National Socialism, particularly between 1930 and 1933, when the Party, then sometimes at odds with its sponsors, made one street collection after the other. The same technique is applied by other American anti-Semitic agitators as well. It would be shortsighted to underestimate the psychological value of the begging attitude. People are generally ready to attribute a higher value to things for which they made financial sacrifices. Money works as a bond. But this does not sufficiently explain why the prospective leader himself, in blatant contradiction to the idea of his grandeur, plays with the aspect of being a beggar. Ambitious men, such as Thomas or Phelps, are certainly more interested in their political career than in their immediate modest financial gains, and they certainly know what they do when they reiterate their clamor for dollars and cents. A tentative explanation would be the universal feeling of insecurity of the masses in the present economic phase. No one but the very rich feels himself as the master of his economic fate any longer but rather as the object of huge blind economic forces working upon him. Everyone senses that he is somehow at the mercy of society; the spectre of the beggar looms behind the psychological imagery of each individual. The fascist agitator reckons with this disposition. By assuming a begging attitude he not only appears on equal footing with those whom he addresses. He also takes it upon himself psychologically to do the begging himself, to undergo psychologically the very same humilation of which his follower is afraid, and thus to "redeem" him symbolically of the shame of being a beggar by assuming this function vicariously and hallowing it, as it were.

As far as Thomas is concerned, the begging attitude often assumes an aspect of metaphysical blackmail, not altogether unlike the "*Ablaß*" technique of the Roman Catholic Church at the beginning of the bourgeois age. He suggests at least indirectly that one may buy the heavenly kingdom by helping him to pay his bills.

We keep a very accurate record of every dollar that is given to this movement, and so we know every penny that comes in and exactly, my friends, where the money comes from and where the money goes. I am appealing for the spirit of God to speak to your heart right now that you have a little part in this great movement that is spreading across America. Remember that we must pay our bills, the petty bills, the stamp bills, remote control bills and radio bills and the office bills.[16]

16 May 23, 1935.

Evidently Thomas reckons with most peoples' complicated psychological attitude towards money – a streak of bad conscience they feel for everything they own – in his attempts to divert the "tithe of God" into his own pockets. He also appeals to the American sense of a good bargain, that everything has its definite price, that everything can be expressed in terms of its financial equivalent. This is, by the way, a line followed by commercial advertisers who expect housewives to buy their soap as the price for their "soap operas." In Thomas this idea is combined with the indefatigability device. "I am sacrificing every ounce of brain energy that I have in this great cause. I am wondering if I could appeal to you, a few people to send in $10."[17] Most important, however, not only does he beg for money, but he also speaks all the time about his financial difficulties and does not refrain from describing himself as someone who undertook larger financial obligations than he actually could fulfill. Therefore, he needs help from his followers who may get a tremendous gratification out of being capable of helping the great little man who has the same worries as themselves. They may even consider themselves his financial superiors. Simultaneously, his acknowledgment of a certain financial incorrectness on his part may appeal to the predatory instinct of his followers.

Thomas' line of propaganda is a characteristic mixture of the pompousness of a man who has to direct big affairs and the cry of the despondent. The following quotation is characteristic of his configuration:

I have come to a crisis in the future of this work. My financial secretary presented me yesterday with a printer's bill, contracted during the month of May, alone, of $800. I am frank to say that I had not known how much that bill had accumulated up. I find that during the month of May, we mailed out practically 100,000 copies of all of this literature. All of the printing bills and the postage bills ran during the month of May twelve hundred dollars alone. Now, I have got to come to a decision between one or two things. I have either got to make a very definite appeal to you people to aid me in materially reducing this bill, or stop at once all mailing. Undoubtedly, I will have to stop sending anything further until this bill is paid. I

17 May 25, 1935.

cannot allow this bill to accumulate. I do not think it is the will of God. I didn't know. I didn't realize that the May bill of printing, the highest in the history of the movement had accumulated so much. Of course, we thank God for it. It only indicates the extent of this movement, but it also indicates, beloved, that you and I must get down on our knees this morning and make this the special order of the day.[18]

He alludes to his having a financial secretary, like an executive, and to his want of $800. Translated into psychological terms, this may mean: I have power rather than money.

The mixture of pettiness and grandeur is not limited to money matters alone. Thomas' whole personal attitude wavers between very small, practical, down-to-earth matters, and grandiose statements which are brought together without any intermediary logical stages. The two are simply identified with each other so that even the poorest listener can feel "elevated" at once from his low status to the realm of ideas. Neither Thomas nor the listener worries about the way that leads from their limited private existence to the spheres of social and religious abstractions. It is a travesty of thought, drawn from an old theological tradition, which is now manipulated in order to profiteer on the narrow-mindedness and disillusioned soberness of the poor by translating high-sounding ideas into their imagery. Thomas' speeches are full of minor technicalities which are linked together with "this great movement" or the spreading of Christianism throughout America. In one of his speeches he gives a circumstantial description of how to reach his church, mentioning even that "officers will be on duty to aid you to and fro across the boulevard" and continues:

Be certain and come tonight. If you are a real Christian and a real American and I know there are thousands of you who are, you are going to be here and we are going to take some action tonight by the blessing of God.[19]

This technique is applied even to the concept of eternal life. It is conceived in terms of the little man who is afraid of all sorts of illnesses. Eternity becomes a sort of life insurance:

18 June 4, 1935.
19 April 14, 1935.

Now do you know what eternal life is? It means forever and forever. It means a life that is unending. It means a life where there will be no death. It means a life where there will never be disease. It means a life where there will never be sorrow.[20]

As soon as his promises are utterly beyond realization within existing society and, hence, are free from any rational control, they become lavish like the day-dreams of the child into whom he wants to transform his listener.

Eternal life means that you and I and every man and woman that accepts the Son of the living God is going on, tens of thousands of years, ten million years, ten billion years, ten trillion years, and you can multiply each of these by ten. It means the ages of the ages. Isn't it worthwhile?[21]

It should be noted that Himmler, in a famous speech, predicted that the Third Reich would last from 20,000 to 30,000 years. To boast about trillions of years of life and then to ask humbly "isn't it worthwhile?" is the most perfect expression of the idea of the "great little man" that Thomas wishes to convey. He combines the ideas of trillions of years and of sound investment. He disposes of eternity and is a reliable broker.

The "great little man" device, the mixture of sublimity and soberness, again is combined with the "indefatigability" device in a sentence that shows utter contempt for any sense of proportion:

Pray that God will put it into the heart and mind of this great living audience that they have no peace night and day until they send for this vital literature that we are sending out free of charge.[22]

He psychologically established an immediate relationship between the demand for his petty pamphlets and the religious peace of the soul. Only if one is indefatigable in asking for "this vital literature" does one have a chance of getting any sleep at all.

20 May 24, 1935.
21 *Ibid.* The inflationary character of those figures may have something to do with the contempt for any established money value inherent in fascism. This mixture of apparently sober figuring and fantastic expectations is utterly unthinkable for the liberalistic mentality, though it may have its precedents in American sectarianism.
22 *Ibid.*

"Human interest"

The audience which Thomas addresses has to be imagined as consisting largely of elderly, somewhat lonesome, disappointed lower-middle-class people, particularly women. This accounts for one of his favorite personal attitudes: the "human interest" trick, the deliberate fiction of personal closeness, warmth, and intimacy. This attitude has proven its value through, for instance, the tremendous appeal of the key figures in women's serials. Thomas presents himself in a sense as the homespun philosopher, the folksy, good-natured, humble man with the golden heart who, although himself by no means living comfortably, thinks of his neighbor first, brings him comfort, and gives him some sort of help. Though the "human interest" device of Thomas is related to his specific audience, it should be noted that it can also be found among a great many American fascist agitators, such as Phelps, while it was largely absent from German Nazi propaganda. Apparently, the pressure of technology and the highly centralized business culture in this country is so tremendous that those who live under this pressure clamor for "strong dope." Radio, of course, with its fake immediateness, bringing the distant voice into the little man's own home, is a particularly adequate medium for this device.

Thomas seems to be capable of speaking with perfect ease about the most intimate matters of his own life to perfect strangers – experiences about which anyone who actually had them would be completely reticent.

God called me. He did not call me until my little mother was on her deathbed. When she called me to her side and said "before you were born into this world I dedicated you to God and I dedicated you to be a minister to the Son of God."[23]

This experience is supposed to have brought about a complete change in his life, a kind of Augustinian conversion. "My life was immediately changed. The things that I loved from the standpoint of the flesh I immediately hated."[24] His whole

23 June 7, 1935.
24 *Ibid.*

family is summoned for propaganda purposes, notwithstanding the fact that his actual family life was by no means happy. He mentions an illness of his wife and asks the community to pray for her, although he hurries to add that "she is not so very ill."[25] When he suffers from a cough, he uses it as a means of achieving a personal touch and appearing as "human," while at the same time stressing his spirit of boundless sacrifice. "Now if I have to cough today, I know that you will forgive me and realize that I am laboring under a tremendous handicap."[26] Correspondingly, he feigns an intimate interest in the family affairs of his listeners. There are always sick people, always people down the hill, always people who suffer under humiliating conditions, and he advertises his sympathy for all of them. "I trust that everybody had a good night's rest, that you are refreshed, and that you are getting ready for a great day tomorrow, as well as today."[27] He shares in their joys no less than in their sorrows and plays upon the pride they take in junior. "Let any man or woman listening to me this morning hour who is not in reality governed by their emotions look into those blue eyes of that baby of yours."[28]

Here the trick is obvious. There are innumerable babies with blue eyes, but to most mothers these eyes appear as an intimate, specific characteristic. By referring to them, Thomas fakes his closeness to those whom he never saw, without any danger of being disavowed.

"Good old time"

One particular form of the "human interest" trick may be called the "good old time" device. It consists of placing special emphasis on the old fashioned and the obsolete in one's actions and surroundings. The American cult of novelty is likely to

25 June 26, 1935.
26 June 6, 1935.
27 May 25, 1935.
28 May 29, 1935.

produce a sort of resentment within all those who cannot participate in the latest blessings of technical civilization, whereas
even to those who participate in modern technology life
appears to become colder and colder by the sweep of progress.
Thomas overcompensates for this feeling by emphasizing the
old-fashioned and the homely as being genuine and traditional
and as having a sort of patina which the novelties lack. Thus,
the patina itself falls within the same advertising pattern as the
novelties do – a scheme familiar from commercial advertising.
In a description of Thomas' church, its lack of glamor is
glamorized.

We don't have much of a church here. We don't have any stained
glass windows. We don't have a great deal of marble and brick. We
just have a little old-fashioned church by this great highway. The total thing did not cost us but $3600, but folks, we love Christ out
here and we are trying to serve him to the very best of our ability.
If you are worn and tired of life and if you think that God does not
live, why don't you come tonight . . . suppose you get that old Bible
of yours. That old Bible that you have loved and that has come
down through the years . . . perhaps it belonged to that old father of
yours or mother or somebody. Go, get it, won't you?[29]

Thomas capitalizes on resentment and frustration by confirm-
ing the homeliness of those who cannot afford nice things as a
morally superior way of life. In addition, the denunciation of
"stained glass windows and marble," which are here a sort of
religious substitute for make-up and lipstick, fits in very well
with his generally ascetic, anti-sensual, and anti-hedonist
attitude, which he has in common with practically all fascist
agitators in the whole world.

The ideal that looms behind the "human interest" trick is
that of the traditionalistic, anti-liberal poor, who, in spite of
their poverty, are content with life as it is and are ready to
sacrifice themselves for the maintenance of the very same
conditions under which they suffer, being rewarded by the
dubious pleasure of some undefined inner superiority over the
rich as well as the discontented. All Thomas' maudlin appeals
aim at establishing this attitude which he regards as the most
promising one to be taken by his peculiar type of listeners.

29 July 7, 1935.

I see coming before me today a great crowd of little women with hard hands from scrubbing the floors, from going over the washtubs. I see a great host of those who have never bowed the knee to Communism in the world. I see this great host of womanhood. Many of them ... saving, praying, working that this magnificent gospel of the son of God shall continue across the world.[30]

To sum up the personal attitude that Thomas pretends to take: he stresses the personal element, the similarity between himself and the audience, and the whole sphere of interest, as a sort of emotional compensation for the cold, self-alienated life of most people and particularly of innumerable isolated individuals of the lower middle classes. The very immediateness and warmth of his approach, furthered by radio, helps him to get a firmer grip over them. The substitute for their isolation and loneliness is not solidarity, but obedience. He advocates obsolescent, quasi-precapitalistic forms of human euphoria against the streamlined conditions of today, in order to prepare for their transformation into something even more streamlined, the totalitarian leader-state. The sham individualism, preached by Thomas, only furthers the tendency to dispose of the individual by incorporating him into a collectivity, where he may feel "sheltered" but where he has no say at all.

30 July 12, 1935.

Section II:
Thomas' Method

Introductory Remarks

A survey of the method used by Thomas in handling his audience, apart from the personal element previously analysed, is important not only because his methods are common to fascist and anti-Semitic agitators whose actual doctrines widely differ, but also for a more specific reason. *With Thomas as with most of his kin, the method, the "how," is more important than the contents, the "what."* His actual interest is the manipulation of men, their transformation into adherents of his organization, and in the last analysis everything serves this purpose. The specific ideas and postulates serve merely as bait and have very little objective weight. Partly, he is too cautious to reveal his real aims. Partly, he presupposes, probably correctly, that the audience understands what he actually advocates, that is, jingoist violence, much better when he deals with political goals in a less explicit way. He obeys an old German chauvinistic rule of the thumb: *Immer daran denken, nie davon reden.* Partly, the goals themselves are vague and inarticulate and will have to be adapted to changing political situations, as soon as the fascist feels himself in command of power. Partly, his followers should not know too exactly what is intended, his political program, for they might discover the blatant discrepancy between their own most primitive interests and the interests which they are called upon to serve. Thus, the emphasis is shifted from the "what" to the "how." Thomas is an advertising expert in a highly specialized field, that of the transformation of religious bigotry into political and racial hatred. He gives much more attention to his advertising techniques than to the ideas which he tries to sell. The psychological stimuli he provides, and the response mechanism on which he reckons, are carefully worked out; his platforms, on the other hand, are either vague and abstract or childish and absurd, and so one has every reason to believe that he knows very well why he devotes more attention to psychological techniques than to concrete political issues. The latter, conversely, enter the picture only on a very down-to-earth, atheoretical level, in terms of election campaigns and scandal mongering, and hence reveal little about his final ends.

In objective terms, Thomas' radio speeches are quite illogical. There is no clear-cut and transparent relationship between premises and inferences, causes and effects, data and concepts. It would be a mistake, however, to attribute this lack of discursive logic to a lack of intellectual capacity. Thomas is a shrewd man. The lack of objective logic in his statements is due to quite logical reflections about the psychology of his listeners and the best way to reach them; and some of his apparently most illogical devices are certainly the result of hard thinking and long experience, although a certain affinity between the speaker's mind and the supposed muddle-headedness of his listeners should not be discounted. As a whole, however, Thomas' radio speeches offer an excellent example for one of the basic characteristics of fascist and anti-Semitic propaganda, namely, the entirely calculated, highly rationalistic nature of its irrationalism, not only with regard to the irrational philosophy that it implies, but also to its irrational effect. Thomas' method may be adequately described as "emotional planning." This is demonstrated first of all by the general strategy of his speeches. They fall into two totally distinct divisions, the "esoteric" and the "exoteric."[1] The esoteric ones are those which were not broadcast, particularly those delivered in Trinity Auditorium. They were addressed to the nucleus of his followers, the people to whom he could speak his mind and whom he could whip up to the peak of

1 The same dichotomy pertains to Hitler's speeches. There is a large difference between his addresses to the old party members and those for the outer world. Incidentally, the distinction between speeches "for home consumption" and others has become quite universal and is almost officially recognized. The logic of manipulation cynically admits different "truths."

emotional hatred. Here alone his anti-Semitic propaganda
went unchecked, and it is these speeches which provide the
key for certain passages of the radio addresses which, subject
to the control of the stations and of public opinion, are soft-
pedalled and avoid abusive statements in most cases. Their
function is to attract people who could be incorporated into his
organization and, of course, to secure money. These exoteric
speeches, to the study of which we confine ourselves here, are
largely to be interpreted as advertising for the non-public,
esoteric activities. These exoteric speeches are carefully balanced.
Whenever Thomas dared a violent political attack, he became mild and harmless in the next utterance; very often
speeches which deal at least in part with political matters are
followed by ones of an apparently purely religious nature. He
follows, purposely or automatically, the Hitlerian "wave
technique" described by Edmond Taylor.[2] He is always
cautious enough to keep open the road for retreat and could
even counterbalance his anti-Semitic statements by appeals
to Gentiles and Jews alike in the Coughlin manner. As a
whole, his speeches may show a certain crescendo in violence
and aggressiveness, due to the increasing scope of his "crusade."
This crescendo, however, is interrupted whenever he meets any
difficulties with public agencies, and it would be hard to
gauge it exactly. By and large, his radio speeches belong to the
realm of indirect, semi-hidden, fascist and anti-Semitic propaganda and most of his techniques can be traced back to his
endeavour to excite hatred and violence without committing
himself. In this respect he is different from many other anti-
Semitic agitators, such as [William Dudley] Pelley. However,
he is shrewd enough to use even his cautious avoidance of
definite commitments as a peculiar kind of threat. Here he is
doubtlessly influenced by Nazi propaganda which always
sounded most dangerous when it stressed the "strict legality"
of its methods and ends.

2 Edmond Taylor, *The Strategy of Terror: Europe's Inner Front* (Boston:
Houghton Mifflin, 1940).

"Movement" trick

The vagueness of Thomas' statements about his political objectives cannot be shown by quotation since it is a negative aspect of his utterances. He defines his aim as something like the concern for the Holiness of God and an ensuing "regeneration" of the world. (The idea of regeneration with the implication of hatred for the "degenerate ones" is common to all anti-Semites since Gobineau and Chamberlain.) The vagueness of this aim itself, however, is shrewdly utilized. The trick consists of substituting the concept of the movement itself for the aim of the movement, an aim that is purposely left vague. The description of the "revival" that he expects has always something redundant, lacking any definite application.

My friend, there is not but one way to get a revival and all America has got to get that revival . . . all of the churches. The story of the great Welsh revival is simply this. Men became desperate for the holiness of God in the world, and they began to pray, and they began to ask God to send a revival (!), and wherever men and women went the revival was on. It was not confined to one church, one area. When men and women came into the outdoors, a great something gripped them to know God. They began to cry out to God, to save their souls.[3]

This description of older revivalist meetings may not be altogether wrong; they consisted in collective imitation, a sort of contagion of ecstasy, rather than in being overwhelmed by any concrete, specific idea. Revival is not a revival for something; it is rather an end in itself, and it is hardly accidental that Thomas describes the Welsh revival as nothing but a universal desire for a revival. This is transferred to Thomas' own political racket. The movement is conceived of as an end in itself, like the Nazis who always made a fetish of the term *Bewegung* without pointing out exactly where the *Bewegung* was going. "This great movement," the glorification of action, of something going on, both obliterates and replaces the purpose of the movement; Thomas becomes very concrete only when dealing with matters of organization and money, or with his adversaries and the danger that is supposed to threaten,

3 July 10, 1935.

but never with regard to any positive idea. This configuration may point to some of the deepest psychological implications of the stimuli that he exhibits to his audience. He wants to evince an "against" rather than a "for" attitude, and the gratification which he psychologically promises by his total approach is, in the last analysis, the pogrom rather than the achievement of any aim apart from such an outbreak. The movement is presented as a value *per se*, because it is understood that movement implies violence, oppression of the weak, and exhibition of one's own power. Since the goal is finally the subjugation of one's own followers, they should be distracted from this goal, and their ambition should be centered around the pleasure which the movement itself may yield, not around the ideas which it might possibly materialize. The shift of the emphasis from end to means is one of the axioms of the logic of fascist manipulation. The end is "that we might demonstrate to the world that there are patriots, God-fearing Christian men and women who are yet willing to give their lives for the cause of God, home and native land."[4] These words, by association, ring like those of the Ku Klux Klan, nativism, and Chauvinism, that is to say, they bear some definite destructive connotations, but remain quite vague apart from such associations. The transformation of means into an end is blatant: "To give their lives for the cause of God" is a means and the end would be only that cause which is never stated concretely. The negative concept of sacrifice remains the last end Thomas has to offer. The means by which it is supposed to be achieved are the Christian American Crusade, its paper, the pamphlets, the money for which Thomas asks. All the weight of his propaganda is thrown in to promote the means. Propaganda is the ultimate content of this propaganda.

"Flight-of-ideas" technique

The lack of any program or goal makes itself felt in the logical structure of Thomas' speeches. Since he has nothing to prove,

4 July 14, 1935.

since no real conclusion is ever to be reached by an analysis of given material, no actual argumentation takes place at all. Yet, Thomas is American enough to reckon with the common sense of his listeners, and he therefore upholds the form of rational thinking, corroborating his theses by examples and apparently making deductions. The inferences, however, are as spurious as the examples. The logical trick consists of the fact that he always takes for granted that his so-called "conclusions" are the pre-existing convictions of every true Christian American. While apparently proving something, he actually only wants to corroborate those common prejudices which agree with his plan. Everything is decided before the argument starts. In his confused ideas there is a sort of totalitarian order. Everything is settled. One knows what is good and bad, which powers are the powers of Christian tradition, family, and native soil, and which are those of baseness, degeneration, and world Bolshevism. No problem exists, no adversary is refuted, no thesis is rationally justified. The logical process merely consists of identification, or rather of pigeonholing. The whole set of values, including even the most doubtful ones, is regarded as pre-established, and the orator's effort is spent entirely in identifying any group, person, race, denomination, or whatever it may be, with one of the rigid concepts of his frame of reference. Even in this process of identification Thomas never takes the trouble to actually prove that any phenomenon belongs rightly to any of those pseudo-logical classes. He feeds upon the bias connected with the phenomenon and expands it by subsuming it under some high-sounding category, such as the forces of evil, the Pharisees, or the Battle of Armageddon. Argumentation has been replaced by the device, termed in the book on Coughlin by the Institute of Propaganda Analysis the "name-calling device."[5] This is grounded not only in the weakness of fascist reasoning itself, which, from the viewpoint of its profiteers, is

[5 The Institute for Propaganda Analysis, *The Fine Art of Propaganda: A Study of Father Coughlin's Speeches*, eds. Alfred McClung Lee and Elizabeth Briant Lee (New York: Harcourt, Brace and Company, 1939) pp. 26-46; 95-104.]

reasonable enough. It is rather based upon a cynical contempt
for the audience's capacity to think – a contempt overtly
expressed by Hitler. Thomas reckons with an audience who
cannot think, that is to say, who is too weak to maintain a
continuous process of making deductions. They are supposed
to live intellectually from moment to moment, as it were, and
to react to isolated, logically unconnected statements, rather
than to any consistent structure of thought. They know what
they want and what they do not want, but they cannot detach
themselves from their own immediate and atomistic reactions.
It is one of the main tricks of Thomas to dignify this atomistic
thinking as a kind of intellectual process. By reproducing in
his speeches the vagueness of a thinking process confined to
mere associations, a *"monologue intérieure,"* Thomas provides
a good intellectual conscience for those who cannot think. He
cunningly substitutes a "paranoic" scheme for a rational
process.

The most important device of his logic of manipulation is his
technique of *associational transitions.* Whether he chooses this
technique deliberately or whether it flows simply from ora-
tional habits, its essence is to connect different sentences, or
ideas, not by any logical operation, but simply by some
element which they have in common and which makes them
appear connected in spite of possibly complete logical dis-
parity. A typical argument which recurs most frequently in
various forms runs as follows:

Christ says, "by their fruits ye shall know them," now, that is the
only way that I have of testing whether a man or woman belongs to
God, it is what you do. My friend, one of the best things in the world
that you can do to demonstrate that you are a child of God-work
on your neighbor; send for all of this vital literature.[6]

The trick is played by the double meaning of the word "neighbor" which serves as associational link. The word "neighbor"
plays a definite role in Christian theological language, and the
idea that "by their fruits ye shall know them" is generally
interpreted as that of doing good works towards one's "neighbor." On the other hand, the word "neighbor" has a plain

6 May 29, 1935.

realistic meaning, referring to the man next door, that is to say, the acquaintance to whom Thomas wants his follower to direct his house-to-house propaganda. The follower should send for "this vital literature" in order to "start a chain, contact your neighbors, have them contact five more people, and keep the chain going"[7] – the notorious chain-letter device, that has certain mischievous connotations in itself. The associational technique consists in bringing closely together the idea of good works and of asking for Thomas' printed pamphlets. In reality, there is no connection between the pamphlets and theological or moral truth; by the word "neighbor" they are wedded to each other.

Another example shows an even more arbitrary connection of ideas:

You know, I see, this morning, yonder on the bleak New England shore, I see that Mayflower, and a little group of men and women, after they have spent three months upon that great uncharted sea, and here is what they are saying: listen to that historic Mayflower compact "in the name of God." You call upon that same God that our fathers called upon, and you call upon the same God to guide us through the storms that we are now moving through, and you also remember, my friend, that the Christian American Crusade cannot possibly go another forty-eight hours unless you, through the power of the Holy Spirit shall make a real sacrificial offering. I cannot possibly go further, my friend, unless I receive during the next twenty-four to thirty-eight hours sufficient money to run this.[8]

The main link is the identical name for something real and something metaphorical. The Mayflower went through real storms; Thomas' racket goes through a financial crisis. Calling the latter a storm, he links his movement to the voyage of the Mayflower and borrows from the prestige of that established American legend. Moreover, the Pilgrim Fathers were religious. So are his followers supposed to be, and religion means sacrifice. Hence, they are called in the name of the Mayflower to send him money.

A last example: "As we know Christ, we enter in, and we go out. We find pastures. Our God provides a pasture for his

7 *Ibid.*
8 June 25, 1935.

sheep. That is the reason this message is going out, today, for it is food for the spiritual lives."[9] Here the associative link is completely formalistic. A central agency sends out identical material simultaneously to innumerable individuals. In the one case it is supposed to be God who spiritually nourished his children; in the other case it is Mr. Thomas who speaks over the radio. The implication of the trick is that by associative transition the message of Thomas is dressed up as a message of God in person – an idea which is helped by the theological language that he constantly employs. It should be noted that this device is closely akin to what is called the "transfer" device in the above-mentioned Coughlin analysis. But the trick implies more than the idea of borrowing prestige from something established and transferring it to something apocryphal and even shabby. Its ultimate aim is probably not so much the selling of a false argumentation as, indeed, the complete breakdown of a logical sense within the listeners and eventually the collapse of any meaning that the idea of truth may have for them. They are trained to accept oratorical expectoration, backed by all the authority which is implied in the attitude of any speaker who addresses a mass, as a sort of command. They are to give up the element of resistance that is implied in any act of responsible thinking as such. They are to follow the leader first intellectually, and finally in person through thick and thin. We may add that this device as well as practically all the others discussed in this study are used hundreds and hundreds of times throughout Thomas' speeches so that they become a kind of a pattern and have a greater chance of being accepted, since they are employed as an established form of intellectual procedure. He has a "style of thinking," the consistency of which throughout its repetition hides the inner inconsistency of each case.

9 July 5, 1935.

"Listen to your leader"

It is a truism that authoritarian propaganda does everything to establish authoritarian ideas. This, taken in isolation, however, is not a specific characteristic of fascism. Other ideologies, particularly religious and feudal-conservative ones, have always dwelt on the concept of authority. The new element in propagating authority is that anti-democratism can no longer refer to authorities which are regarded either as being guaranteed by supernatural revelation, such as the Church, or as being grounded in an omnipresent tradition, such as the "legitimistic" idea of feudal authority and, to a certain extent, even of monarchism. Modern authoritarianism has to face an issue which first came into the open in the period of French Restoration, in the writings of reactionaries, such as Bonald and de Maistre. Throughout modern society the problem is conspicuously manifested. The fascist must try to justify authoritarianism which is an inherent tendency of modern industrial organization. Yet he must face ways of thought which are essentially opposed to authority itself, and must confront those very masses which are to be subdued by authority. This task, essentially insoluble, calls for certain twists and distortions if it is to be undertaken with any chance of success.

Most of the techniques of rationalistically and "democratically" defending blind authority are hackneyed and have often been exposed. Typical is the "transfer" device described in the Coughlin study of the Institute of Propaganda Analysis,[10] a device which consists of transferring the established popular authority of a faith, an idea, or a person to the thesis which the fascist wants to invest with the halo of authority. Or we may mention the equally well-known "Bandwagon" device, which aims at luring people to join one's movement by pretending that a vast number of other people already have done so. We shall not once more describe these devices which are incessantly employed by Thomas.[11] Rather, we confine

[10 Lee and Lee, *The Fine Art of Propaganda*.]
11 At least a few examples for these devices may be given.
Transfer. "From all indication, there is arising in this country a great

ourselves to discussing some tricks which have not yet been fully recognized, and to considering the broader psychological background of modern fake authority as such.

The most characteristic means of propagandistically establishing authority in a quasi-rational way, without taking resort to traditionally accepted institutions, consists of taking up an authoritarian term and making it a sort of fetish. This device has been noted by Dr. A. Sanders[12] under the heading of "magic words." The best example for this device is the personification of totalitarian regimes everywhere, by a *Duce*, a

crusade of Christian American Crusaders and that is we can continue another twelve months over this station and a national hookup, that this movement alone will save the United States. In the words of ex-President Hoover, yesterday, he said that, 'America has a responsibility to the world far beyond the boundaries of our own land, so far as democracy and representative form of government is concerned and the maintaining of a religious freedom upon the part of an individual.' My friend, our ex-President is correct: Unless you people will guard the freedom that our forefathers have given to us . . ." (July 5, 1935). The quotation from Hoover is a commonplace statement about America's international responsibilities which any statesman might make at any time. By coupling it with an assertion that his organization will save the United States, however, Thomas makes it appear that Hoover would endorse the Christian American Crusade. Actually, of course, the agreement applies to a notion so abstract that practically everyone would concur. The authority of Herbert Hoover, who is not accidentally quoted as "ex-President," is psychologically transferred to Thomas' group by the intermediary link of agreement with regard to some vague generalities. There is not the faintest proof that Hoover actually was in sympathy with Thomas' propaganda.

Band wagon. Every letter Thomas receives is presented as an index of the avalanche-like character of his movement: "Here is one from Ohio, showing the extent of the movement that is reaching out over this station, another from Kentucky ordering quantities of the literature, another from Nebraska, another from Oklahoma and another from Oregon. Now, I just tell that in order to let you folks know the extent that this thing is going" (June 12, 1935). In one characteristic example the band wagon idea is combined with a metaphor of destructive violence: "I have in my hand about eight or ten letters. Here is one from a sister down in Compton. She says: 'I am glad that you are firing a shot heard around the United States of America'" (June 12, 1935).

12 A. Sanders, "Social Ideas in McGuffey Readers," *Public Opinion Quarterly* V, 4 (fall, 1941), pp. 579-589.

Führer, or, with Martin Luther Thomas, a leader.[13] The term leader itself is very significant in this respect. It expresses a claim of unquestioned authority, the claim that the leader should be "followed" without referring to any traditional dynastic title. Hitler's propagandistic instinct in this respect is so outspoken that he did not even assume the title of *Reichspräsident* after Hindenburg's death in 1934. Hitler called himself the leader of the whole of the German people. The leader is he who ought to be obeyed blindly and only for the sake of his own merits, which are supposed to be self-evident and appreciated by all. His psychological status is paradoxical: It combines irrational devotion on the part of his followers with the rationality that he is actually best equipped to do the job and that the followers should recognize him as best. Here, no doubt, the model of the military officer has been transferred to the realm of politics and emancipated from any idea of expertness and organized control. The *Führer* is *per se* the officer against whose decisions no objection is possible. The term leader expresses its emancipation by becoming absolute.

Current opinion about fascism would object that the concept of the leader, taken as an absolute, is entirely irrational and in no way different from any other magical idolatry of human beings. This idea is furthered by legalistic Nazi constructions such as that of the *charisma of the Führer*. While the ultimate irrationality and arbitrariness of the leader idea, however, is indisputable, one would oversimplify things and therewith

13 All three terms have exactly the same meaning. Moreover, they all have a certain bourgeois ring and carry no association of nobility. The Latin word *dux* fairly early was applied to feudal war lords (*Herzöge*) and so lost its original functional reference to one who draws others behind him. This feudal notion of a *dux qua Herzog* is expressed in Italian by *duca*. Mussolini consciously went back to the original functional meaning by calling himself not *duca* but *Duce*. With the leader charisma becomes a profession, a kind of work that must be done.

Incidentally, traces of anti-feudal authoritarianism can be found in Richard Wagner. His *Rienzi* calls himself, significantly enough, "tribune," a title referring to the Roman representative of the *plebs*, and *Lohengrin* is called *Schützer von Brabant*, Protector of Brabant. Protector later became a Nazi title bestowed upon the notorious Heydrich. The affinity of such traits to the "messenger device" should not be overlooked.

make them too harmless by immediately referring to this
ultimate irrationality and thus dismissing the whole leader
ideology as pure nonsense. Two facts are to be borne in mind.
First, the concentration of economic power in certain nations
has reached such a level that those who hold such power
actually exercise what amounts to absolute authority within a
"rational" industrial society. Second, the potential strength of
the underlying population makes itself felt insofar as the
authoritarian leaders are compelled to justify their usefulness
in some way to those whom they command. This state of affairs
leads to the paradoxical construction of the *Führer* as an
absolute yet somehow "responsible" authority. The social
conflict that stands behind this construction and, as it were,
calls for it, invests the *Führer* principle with an inner strength
which is comparatively immune with regard to its inherent
logical inconsistencies.

The idolatry of the term leader itself is not simply a relapse
into barbarian habits of thought, though it doubtlessly implies
retrogressive elements. It is in itself the outcome of late industrial society in a way which at least may be hinted at. The
intermediary between industrial rationality and magical idolatry is advertising. The technique of competition has developed
a certain tendency to turn the slogans under which the
commodities are sold into magical ones. Such magic of the
words is promoted by incessant and omnipresent repetition
which is planned rationally but blunts the conscious discrimina-
tion of the prospective customers. An important element in
this process is that the customers feel the tremendous power
concentrated behind the ever-repeated words and therefore
display a certain psychological readiness to obey. This obedience tends to a certain extent to sever the link between the
customers' own interest and the actual usefulness of the
commodity. They come to attribute to the product a certain
value *per se,* a certain fetish character. This mechanism has
become so automatized throughout the buying processes of
modern life that it can easily be transferred by simple advertising techniques to the political field. The mode of "selling an
idea" is not essentially different from the mode of selling a

soap or a soft drink. Sociopsychologically, the magical character of the word leader and therewith the *charisma* of the *Führer* is nothing but the spell of commercial slogans taken over by the agencies of immediate political power.

Thomas' speeches contain a striking example of the process of severing the concept of the *Führer* from any rational context and making it an absolute, a fetish. It matters little who the leaders are. Leadership as such is an ideal, and a man who speaks with authority should be followed. Thomas says in one of his isolationist ventures:

You take Harry Carr in the *Los Angeles Times*, today. You read what he has to say on the first page. We are living in a tremendous hour, when a great world war is immanent. It is here, he says. He speaks of the fact of China being swallowed and being taken over by Japan. He says if America so much as raises a finger in protest, it means war. If Britain so much as raises a finger in protest, it means war. He tells us that Japan by her action in taking over Northern China has served notice to the world that the Orient is through, so far as the rule of the white man is concerned. Why does not the world listen to these men? If they won't listen to Christ and the Bible, why don't they listen to their leaders?[14]

The last passage is a very significant slip of the tongue. He implicitly admits that religious authority has passed away and silently transfers the authority to today's "leaders." Those who hold power are regarded as rightful heirs to divine and absolute authority, precisely and only because they are "leaders," because they hold power. This is the point where the ultimate irrationality of the leader idea becomes blatant. Counterpropaganda should dwell upon this point by elaborating that fascism justifies leadership by nothing but leadership, that admiration of power is more important in the fascist setup than anything else, particularly than its supposed nationalism (a fact that becomes very clear in the last quotation from Thomas), and finally that not only those who fulfill the deified function of the leader but also, correspondingly, the enemies, are interchangeable: the same isolationist groups for whom Thomas spoke in 1935 and who at that time took an implicitly pro-Japanese stand are those who today want the

14 June 14, 1935.

whole war effort to be shifted against Japan, now regarded as
the arch enemy.

In some passages Thomas shows more concretely his conception
of the leader. It resembles very clearly that of the Nordic,
Nazi type with poise, *"Haltung."* It suggests certain virile or
quasi-heroic qualities, especially the absence of mercy, through
metaphors so strongly evoking the idea of archaic prowess that
they contradict the idea of Christian compassion, though
Thomas' image of the leader is supposed to appeal to some
sort of Christian elite:

I am looking for men who have the courage of their convictions. I am
looking for women who have the courage of their convictions. I am
looking for young life, young Americans, thank God, with clear
eyes and clear principles. Young men, stalwart Americans, I am
looking for young women who see straight and think straight, and,
thank God, are willing to act straight, who are not afraid to advance
their opinions, who are not afraid to say yes, I would die for the old
flag of my nation, who are not unwilling to take their place in the
firing line and defend by their lives, yes by their lifeblood, if necessary, this great institution.[15]

Apart from being a leader, the leader has to be a warrior,
ready to fight and die. This readiness is praised as a quality
in itself, independent of any specific contents for which one
has to die, and is linked up with a very general notion of
"this great institution."

Excursus on "fait accompli" technique

It appears to us that such well-known devices as that of psychologically transferring the idea of established authority to
one's own racket, or the band wagon appeal – "two million
customers cannot be wrong" – as well as making into fetishes
certain words, such as "leader," are but special cases of a
much broader pattern underlying all fascist propaganda, at
least in this country. It may be called the *"fait accompli"*
technique. It consists of presenting an issue as one that previously has been decided. The foregone decision is attributed

15 June 9, 1935.

either to the masses who back the speaker's stand, or to the personal and institutional authority on whose prestige he draws, or at least to a clear-cut superiority in the realm of ideas which has simply to be translated into practical, technical terms. Some obvious reasons for this technique lie at hand. On the one hand, it calls for less independence and moral courage to join the party that is already winning. This advantage counts heavily in a situation where the propagandist has to reckon with vast numbers of people who are unwilling to take any real risks, since they live under conditions which make them thoroughly dependent on the stronger ones. On the other hand, belief that the causes have already been decided tends to render any resistance psychologically a hopeless undertaking. The terrorising effect is enhanced by the fact that all fascism involves *numerus clausus* and elite ideas, so that those who come too late have serious reasons to fear disadvantage when the fascist regime is established.[16] They join the band wagon because they do not want to miss the bus.

Of course, the "*fait accompli*" technique, which in many cases assumes silly and fraudulent forms, could hardly work unless it had some basis in reality as well as in the psychology of the people. As to the former, it is true that the present organization of economy actually tends to make people to a very large extent objects of processes which they often fail to understand and which are utterly beyond their control. The dwindling of economic free enterprise and initiative makes life appear to most people as something that happens to them rather than as something which they determine by their own free will. To most people their life actually *is* decided in advance. As soon as there appears an organization which evokes the idea of some strong backing by the powers that be, and which promises something to its followers, great numbers may be willing to transform their vague awareness of being mere objects into adherence to such a movement. Thus they may turn the hateful idea of being thoroughly dependent into

16 Cf. the role played by the concept of the old "party comrades" in Germany and the scorn with which Goebbels treated those who joined the party after March 1933.

an asset, namely, into the belief that by giving up their own will they join the very institution whose victory is predetermined. The "*fait accompli*" technique thus touches upon one of the central mechanisms of the mass psychology of fascism: the transformation of the feeling of one's own impotence into a feeling of strength. The feeling of impotence is represented by the idea that the issue already has been decided without one's having had any say in it; but acknowledgment of this very fact, by "going over" to the established victor, mysteriously and irrationally changes the feeling of impotence into one of power. It is probably the most important task of counterpropaganda to interfere with this mechanism and to demonstrate strikingly to the masses that the mere acknowledgment of impotence, the mere giving up of oneself, by no means entails actual strength and social reward. The manipulation of this whole mechanism, by the way, is by no means limited to fascist propaganda, but is set in motion throughout modern mass culture, particularly in the cinema. A fascist propagandist utilizing this mechanism can rely on processes which to a certain extent have been already automatized. Under this viewpoint even the apparently most harmless movie comedian may unconsciously serve the most sinister purposes of domination.

However, involved in that mechanism there seems to be an element which pertains to even deeper psychological processes, and which may set the stage for the more obvious effects. Here, we can hint at it only in rather general terms. We mean the widespread tendency of present society to accept and even to adore the existent – that which *is* anyway. The processes of enlightenment, the spirit of positivism in its broadest sense, have destroyed magical and "supernatural" ideas by confrontation with empirical reality, with that which exists. In America in particular the conviction prevails that truth is only that which can be verified be referring to facts. Throughout the modern history of the mind, the concept of the factual itself has proved to be stronger than any metaphysical entity. This historical superiority is one of many other factors. We mentioned here only the survival of magical psychological traits after the abolition of metaphysical ideas, the tremendous power over the individual, of today's highly organized social existence, and the ultimate opaqueness and even irrationality of the existent order itself. All this has tended to invest the factual itself with that very halo against which the idea of fact was originally coined. One may go so far as to say that religion largely and unconsciously has been replaced by a very abstract yet tremendously powerful cult of the existent. That something exists is taken as a proof that it is stronger than that which does not exist, and that therefore it is better. One can hardly overrate the extent to which what may be called philosophical Darwinism has permeated every channel of modern psychology. The "*fait accompli*" technique exploits this disposition. By investing anything that is propagated or desired with the quality of existence, this device tends to make it an object of adoration in a sense similar to that in which half-grown boys adore motor cars or airplanes. This adoration of the existent becomes stronger, the more the existent itself is presented in terms of technical rationality and practicability. Insight into these possibilities, as will be seen later, is fully utilized by Thomas. The idea that existence is largely taken as its own justification leads back to the point of departure of our discussion of the leader device, namely, that the term leader as such, void of any justification, be it rational or traditional, is accepted and glorified. When Thomas asks the astonishingly general question "why people don't follow their leaders" the basic assumption behind his cult of the leader is not only, as we pointed out, that power authorizes the leader but probably that even the mere existence of leadership as such, warranted through history, is a sufficient legitimation for the existence of leaders. At this point fascist propaganda is profoundly interconnected with basic trends of modern cultural anthropology. It may be added that it can be fought with more than ephemeral success only if the magification [*sic*] of the existent is finally overcome at its foundation in our present setup. The irrationality of the fascist's delight in the "accomplished fact" idea in general, and in that of established leadership in particular, is but the last consequence of the common sense idea that nothing succeeds like success. The absurdity of fascism can be exploded only if the apparent reasonableness of such ideas is exploded, too.

As far as Thomas is concerned, the *"fait accompli"* technique, apart from his crude application of the "band wagon," the "transfer" and similar devices, comes to the fore in the configurations of his language rather than in the contents of his arguments. His movement was, after all, too limited to allow for large scale *"fait accompli"* propaganda, such as the Nazis used between 1930 and 1933. Conversely, the expression of the *"fait accompli"* idea by mere linguistic forms rather than by disputable assertions about already achieved successes may be less subject to rational control, and therewith more effective. We mention some of the most typical and ever recurring *"fait accompli"* formulas of Thomas' language. He generally speaks of his "crusade" as "this movement," "the great movement," "this thing," as if it were well known to his listeners. He takes it for granted, as it were, treating it as a well established institution, thus relieving himself of the necessity of ever concretely stating what it actually proposes. The threatening and sinister undertone of the term "this movement" should not be overheard. It is so awe inspiring that it cannot even be called by its name. Similarly, Thomas always refers to his pamphlets as "this vital literature." His newspaper, the *"Christian American Crusader,"* is called the "official" newspaper of his movement. This has a double implication. On the one hand, it is suggested that some unauthorized people, perhaps "those sinister forces" or some competitive group, may illegitimately speak for the "crusade" whereas only his paper is the real McCoy and anything else a cheap imitation – an idea obviously borrowed from commercial advertising. On the other hand, the term "official newspaper" conveys the idea that the newspaper and the organization behind it have legitimate, and possibly even governmental authority. In other words, the final aim, the seizure of power, is psychologically hinted at as something largely accomplished. All fascist movements have a tendency to represent themselves as authority supplementary to and opposed to the actual government, as valid organizations supplementary to the still prevailing organization of society, ready to replace the latter at any given time. There is an uninterrupted chain of ideas from the "official" newspaper of a small political racket to the huge para-military organizations, to wit, the private armies of the Nazis before 1933. The American term "self-styled" or "self-appointed" authority very clearly delineates this device. It is significant, however, that it had to be characterized by a standard term. The trick to make particularistic or private undertakings appear as public, established institutions has become an institution itself. This may well indicate how deeply rooted in modern society is the tendency towards self-appointed officialdom.

"Unity" trick

In Germany one of the most successful Nazi slogans was that directed against the supposedly innumerable parties. Inner disunity was made responsible for the crises of the Weimar Republic, particularly for its inability to build up a sound parliamentary majority during its last years. This German device proved effective even abroad. It was said often in this country that a democracy with twenty or thirty parliamentary parties could not possibly operate. From the very beginning the whole concept was based upon a lie. Most of the supposedly pernicious parties never played any decisive role, and the number of those which were of any importance was never greater than six or seven. In this country in spite of its age-old and thoroughly established two-party system it is interesting to note that this trick and the appeal for unity as a cloak for totalitarian repressive comprehensiveness is also to be heard; Thomas uses it lavishly. The psychological appeal to unity counts heavier than the actual existence of chaos. The concept of unity itself, as used in this particular device, is void of any specific content. Unity as such is exalted as an idea. The formalism of this ideal makes it possible to put it surreptitiously into the service of the most sinister purposes. On the one hand, the disunity of American society, particularly in politics and religious life, is solemnly decried, and unity is praised as the only hope for salvation from the ever threatening anarchy. On the other hand, Thomas' own organization with all the characteristics of a party is supposed to represent such a unity, or at least to aim at it. Thomas' propaganda betrays one of the innermost features of fascism, namely, the establishment of something utterly limited and particularistic as the totality, the whole, the community. He feeds upon the everpresent feeling of every man that no true solidarity exists in this society, but he directs these feelings into the channels of very specific interests, antagonistic to such a solidarity – the interest of his racket.

He specializes in denouncing jealousy and pleading for unity, but always in a way that justifies certain basic forms of disunity, particularly the prevailing differences of property and social status.

My friend, may I once again re-emphasize through the power of the Holy Ghost that there is no place for jealousy, no place for misunderstanding so far as the Church of God is concerned. You are placed in those places, you cannot choose them. Now, everybody cannot be an officer. Everybody cannot lead the parade, so to speak, but there is just as much honor, yea, more honor to the man or woman who fills the small place in the army as the general who directs the battle. It is just as important, my friend, that God says it is just as much honor and there will be just as great reward as for those who lead things as those who join the battle. We are to be faithful in the place or the places where God has placed us.[17]

The pledge for unity is characteristically mixed up with defamation of theological controversies:

Now, our Lord would not be a party to any jealousy. He would not be a party to encroaching upon the ministry of John. You recall that an attempt had been made by the Pharisees to drive a wedge between the disciples to get them fussing between themselves. You know, my friend, that is always one of the splendid weapons that the Devil uses whenever God takes a great work. Very often it occurs between two ministers.[18]

17 May 23, 1935.
18 May 25, 1935.

Thomas' attack on American denominationalism, which will be discussed later, serves as a sort of metaphor for the dream of political "integration" which is never stated quite explicitly. Sometimes the "unity" device even rings a pro-democratic and antidiscriminatory note:

The thing that the world must see today is the everlasting, pulsating personality of Jesus Christ through God, the Holy Ghost, that is here, today, this hour, that rules every man and woman irrespective of your group, your skin color; it matters not what it may be, you and I come alike and we go alike and six feet of earth makes us alike. Whether you are a poor man or rich, Jew or Gentile, it matters not. There is one God in all, through all and over all.[19]

It is significant, however, that this ideal of equality refers only to supra-natural concepts, namely to the equality before God or before death. The belief in such entities is supposed to work as an integrative force, but the idea of realizing equality on earth is utterly alien to Thomas' propaganda.

My friend, you know what Christianity does. Christianity breaks down all race prejudice. Christianity breaks down all class consciousness; Christianity breaks down all economic barriers. Now, I am talking about a spiritual, a spiritual thing. I do not care tonight (!), whether your skin is dark or white or brown or yellow. If you accept my Father through Jesus Christ my Lord, then you are indeed my brother. Now, that does not mean to say that I believe in intermarriage. I do not. I believe that the black people would be better off marrying within their own. I believe the whites would be better off marrying within their race. I believe the yellow people in their race, because God has set it in our boundaries, within the scope of this earth of ours; but listen, if we can even once get Christ across to this world of ours, the whole question of war is going to be settled; the whole question of an economic war is going to be settled; the whole question of Communism in this nation is going to be settled.[20]

The more firmly the idea of ultimate unity is established as an ideology, the easier it is to maintain any kind of inequality within empirical life.

The "unity" device can easily be recognized as a trick by its exclusiveness. While Thomas speaks about unity in high terms, he always presupposes the existence of certain groups, "those evil forces": the Communists, the radicals, the sceptics, and, of

19 May 26, 1935.
20 April 25, 1935.

course, the Jews. These groups are *a priori* exempted from such a unity; they merely threaten it and must be "driven away." Not one word ever suggests even the faintest possibility of including them in this spiritual unity, be it by conversion or by any other means. They are condemned and have to stay out. Thus, the unity that he advocates is nothing but the ideal of a comprehensive organization of those who participate in his repressive interests, the "right people."

The "democratic cloak"

Thomas' authoritarianism like that of most American Fascist agitators differs in one important aspect from Nazi propaganda. Although some Nazis, such as Schacht, sometimes indulged in defending National Socialism as a true form of democracy, Hitler and his henchmen could openly attack democracy as such. The strength of democratic tradition in America makes this impossible. The famous saying of Huey Long's, that if there ever should be fascism in America, it would be called antifascism, goes for all of his kin. The American attack on democracy usually takes place in the name of democracy. Very often the progressive Roosevelt administration is blamed for being that very dictatorship at which the fascist aims. Thomas, as well as Coughlin, speaks as if he were opposed to all types of dictatorship. However, his critique of dictatorship shows overtones at least of admiration of their successes.

In Europe they are actually regimented, the people, by dictatorship. A regimentation has sprung up such as the world has never known for two thousand years, since Caesar, and they are successful(!). There is hardly a nation in the world, today, with the exeption of the British Commonwealth and America, that does not, today, possess a dictatorship that is leading the people with saddle and spurs and bridle. The people of the world, today, are regimented and bound together. They are bound servants and slaves of their masters above them. Now, why is that? Now, I tell you why it is, because of the fact that there is no soul freedom. No man or woman is ever bound in, today, until they are bound outwardly, rather until they are first bound in.[21]

While this somewhat confused statement seems to complain of

21 June 19, 1935.

the rise of dictatorship, it explains it by the rather vague concept of a preceding loss of "soul freedom." He makes dictatorship an issue of inwardness rather than of politics and economy. It is, according to Thomas, due to a negative frame of mind, antagonistic to his type of religion. That frame of mind – the Nazis would have called it "materialistic" – is supposed to be universal. Thus, by implication, the trend towards fascism is presented as being universal, too. The listener is left under the general impression that there is a compulsion in the drift toward dictatorship. It appears to be the only rescue to obey the authority of Thomas himself. Authoritarianism yields only to authority.

Yet, Thomas' persistent references to democracy, to democratic personalities, such as Jackson or Lincoln, and to the American Constitution is exceedingly significant from the point of view of counterpropaganda. He even pretends that his "great movement . . . is attempting to protect and preserve our ancient liberties."[22] This shows that the fascist agitator still has to reckon with democratic ideas as living forces and that he has a chance for success only by perverting them for his own purposes. By perverting them, however, he is always bound to hurt the very feelings which he wants to utilize. Hence, counterpropaganda should point out as concretely as possible in every case the distortions of democratic ideas which take place in the name of democracy. The proof of such distortions would be one of the most effective weapons for defending democracy.

There is a definite procedure for the perpetration of such distortions, a specific twist by which psychological patterns of democracy are transformed into ideological means of fascism. This procedure is mentioned in the Coughlin study by the Institute of Propaganda Analysis under the title of the "Plain Folks Device."[23] However, little emphasis is laid upon it and it appears in too harmless a light.[24] The "plain folks" device is closely akin to the "good old time" idea discussed in Section

22 April, 1935.
23 Lee and Lee, *The Fine Art of Propaganda*, pp. 92–93.
24 Cf. the assertion that it "serves well many another democratic and

I. But not only the illusion of closeness, warmth, and intimacy is brought about by some pertinent oratory habits well developed in Thomas, such as addressing the listeners and their families as "folks" or exalting certain homely virtues, such as thrift. Behind the veneer of democratic equality, of being affable and not regarding oneself as something better, looms an aggressive "anti-highbrow" attitude in favor of a carefully calculated image of the common man with sound instincts and little sophistication – an attitude zealously fostered by the Nazi denunciation of the intellectual. The fact that American tradition is intrinsically bound up with democratic ideas and institutions has tended to give to some elements of democracy a quasi-magical halo, an irrational weight of their own. Wholesome as this may be in some respects, it also involves certain dangers upon which fascist propaganda may feed, just as it fed in Germany upon certain undercurrents of the idea of the immediate will of the "folks" vs. its alienated (*volksfremd*) expression through government by representation. Such a danger applies particularly to the concept of majority which not only reflects American democracy but is also constantly promoted by the almost universal statistical approach to any social problem, and by the practices of advertising. Whereas in a democracy decisions are to be taken on a majority basis, majority as such is not a moral value but a formal principle of government. It tends, however, to become hypostatized in this country as an end in itself rather than as a means. Thus, certain traits of the population which are due to socially nondemocratic processes, and antidemocratic in spirit, may be taken and propagated as the last word in democracy, simply because they are characteristics of the majority. This is one of the weaknesses which sometimes allow fascism to mobilize the masses for repressive aims against their actual interests.

republican politicians both for socially desirable and undesirable purposes" (*Ibid*). The purposes may sometimes be desirable but still the psychological implications of the device itself are pernicious. It establishes conformism as a moral principle and Mr. Average as a superior person simply because he is average. It is intrinsically related to the resentment against anyone who is different and hence virtually directed against any minority group.

On the surface the "plain folks" device appears to be innocuous enough, and it is by no means a characteristic of fascist agitators to flatter the people as they are. One might assume that such a psychological treatment cures the little men and women of their inferiority complexes and elevates their unvoluntarily humble lives, e.g., by inferring, as Thomas does, that the humbleness is self-imposed out of Christian humility. Yet this device has most sinister implications. It reflects the fact that large sectors of the population – in fact, all those who are excluded from the privilege of education, and through manual labor, bear the burden of civilization – preserve certain traits of rudeness and even of savagery which may be called upon in any critical situation. By praising their humbleness and their folksy ways, the agitator indirectly praises this savagery which is simultaneously both repressed and generated by modern culture. Thus, he leads them to release their savagery under the name of robust, sound, plain instincts. Whenever a group is gathered under the slogan of being "just plain folks" who are opposed to the refinements and perversions of cultural life, it is ready to strike at those against whom they may be directed to strike.

"If you only knew"

The following group of five devices pertains to Thomas' "strategy of terror." Here he enters the sphere of the dark, mysterious and frightening, and resorts to techniques which exploit fear and its ambivalence. The terror technique is used in different degrees, from the slight innuendo of hidden evil to the threat of impending catastrophe. Each of these grades has somewhat different psychological implications.

One has to distinguish, throughout Thomas' method, between the quasi-rational, surface stimuli and the underlying irrational psychological mechanisms which he sets in motion. The difference between these two aspects is particularly marked with regard to the terror device. Here the statements themselves and the emotions they first call forth are of a distinctly negative nature. Simultaneously the whole technique aims at giving or promising certain unconscious gratifications as supplementary effects of the negative statements. Since the actual result is probably an amalgam of surface reactions and deeper psychological implications, we shall try to elaborate both and to show how they are related to each other.

The mildest form of terror device employed by Thomas as well as by other fascists is the "if you only knew" device, the suggestion of mysterious dangers known only to the speaker, or almost unconceivable to the normal person, or so obscene that they cannot be discussed in public.

Innuendo points toward the future, to a time when the facts merely hinted at are going to be made clear, or to a final day of reckoning. Curiosity is stirred up and people are made to join the organization, or at least to read its publications, by the hope that they are going to be "let in" at some future date if they simply follow what the agitator says and writes. Mere interest in what one will hear later creates a sort of emotional tie between speaker and listener. This mechanism is used throughout advertising, and represents the harmless, surface aspect of the innuendo technique.

The lure of innuendo grows with its vagueness. It allows for an unchecked play of the imagination and invites all sorts of speculation, enhanced by the fact that masses today, because they feel themselves to be objects of social processes, are anxious to learn what is going on behind the scene. At the same time they are prone psychologically to transform the anonymous processes to which they are subject into personalistic terms of conspiracies, plots by evil powers, secret international organizations, etc. The innuendo device is based upon the neurotic curiosity prevailing within modern mass culture. Every isolated individual longs not only to know the hidden powers which his existence obeys, but even more to know the dark and sinister side of those lives in which he cannot take part. This disposition helps to transform the innuendo device into something not at all harmless.

Its dangerous aspect consists, first of all, in an irrational increase of the speaker's prestige and authority. To listen to innuendo and to rely on purposely vague statements requires from the listeners a certain readiness to "believe," since the vagueness stands in the way of a comprehensive statement of facts and a discursive treatment of their interrelation. It is exactly this attitude of blind belief which is fostered by Thomas' innuendo technique. Of course, he borrows the concept of belief from Protestant religion, which teaches the primacy of faith. But actually he promotes the idea of belief in *him*. Religious belief and belief in the movement are permanently confused: "God can only bless the world in proportion to that which they [*sic*] yield to Christ. To believe is necessary. Do you believe that God is blessing the Nation through this movement?"[25] Innuendo is a means of making the leader appear as heir to divine omniscience. He knows what the others do not know. He underscores this difference by never telling exactly what he does know or revealing the full extent of his knowledge. He always reserves for himself a surplus of knowledge which inspires awe and at the same time makes the public wish to participate in it.

This is the decisive mechanism of the "if you only knew" device. The assertion that fascist organizations like Thomas' Crusade are rackets is to be taken very seriously. It does not refer merely to the habitual participation of criminals in such movements, nor to their violent terroristic practices. It emphasizes their sociological structure as such: they are repressive, exclusive and more or less secret ingroups. One has every reason to assume that this aspect of any fascist movement is, though unconsciously, well understood by the prospective followers. Indeed, one of the main incentives offered to them is the wish to "belong," to become a member of a closed ingroup. This mechanism is evident in the attraction exercised by juvenile gangs upon youth, and probably also even upon adults. The "if you only knew" device is of paramount importance with regard to this desire. Innuendo is a psychological means of making people feel that they already are members of that closed group which strives to catch them. The assumption that one understands something which is not plain-

25 June 11, 1935.

ly said, a winking of the eye, as it were, presupposes a kind
of esoteric "intelligence" which tends to make accomplices of
speaker and listener.[26] The overtone of this "intelligence" is
invariably a threatening one. Psychologically, what purposely
remains unsaid is not only the knowledge which is too horrible
to be stated frankly but also the horrible thing which one
wants to commit oneself, which is not confessed even to
oneself, and yet is expressed and even sanctioned by innuendo.
The "if you only know" device promises to reveal the secret
to those who join the racket and pay their tithe. But it also
implies the promise that they will some day participate in the
night of long knives, the Utopia of the racket.

Moreover, the form of innuendo is a threat to all those who
are excluded from the whispering and are supposed *not* to
know "what I mean." This idea is often expressed by anti-
Semitic leaflets which demand of their readers that the
material be passed to "Gentiles only."

A typical statement of the "if you only knew" type is the
following:

God has been speaking to this nation. He has been speaking a long
time, but the nation would not listen. They did not hear. The
preachers turned from God. Oh, I don't mean all of them, of
course, but I mean, you know who I mean, a lot of people turned
from God, the businessmen turned from God, God has wept all
these years for America to return to hear: now, judgment has come.
He has allowed radical Communism to come in. My friend, you find
it everywhere.[27]

But although the foe is everywhere he does not come out into
the open; he remains hidden just as the meaning of Thomas'
accusation is hidden by innuendo. While Thomas, like all
fascists, stresses the black-and-white dichotomy between friend
and enemy, psychologically both categories change into each
other. The confusion among them is likely to work as a stimulus
on the ambivalent feelings of the listener.

26 This is particularly true of all kinds of anti-Semitic statements. Lewis
Browne has symbolized this device by the title of his book: *See What I
Mean?* (New York: Random House, 1943).
27 July 7, 1935.

The Devil is a coward. He works in the corner, in the dark places and behind closed doors and walls; but Jesus, thank God, works in the light of the day. Now, I want you to note a purely dastardly political address. God always picks these evil forces and compels them to do in the very light of the day that which they desired to do in the dead of midnight.[28]

This divine action is actually what Thomas constantly promises to do himself, namely to publicly expose the evil forces. But he prefers to do it by innuendo, as it were, "behind closed doors and walls."

My friend, throughout the United States, today, wherever men and women are preaching the Gospel of the Son of God, and wherever they are calling attention to the imminent peril of Communism, there we find the clergy being attacked and you find forces being used to discredit the leaders. Just now, according to the newspapers of last night, you find in Southern California where a tremendous program has been put on and financed by a certain force to discredit every leading clergyman in Southern California, and where they have financed these men to attack the outstanding clergymen in Southern California.[29]

Such a statement is certainly not less dark than the corners of "those evil forces." It may safely be assumed that the basic understanding between Thomas and his listeners, wherever he uses innuendo, refers to the Jews: they are the "certain forces." The threat against them is emphasized by the very fact that he avoids the word "Jew" in his exoteric addresses, while mentioning Communists and radicals, and calls them only "these forces." He implies that everyone knows who and what they are, that it is not even necessary to speak about them. They appear doomed in advance. Thus even the fact that in a democracy open anti-Semitic statements are somewhat handicapped by official public opinion is changed into an anti-Semitic tool of its own.

28 July 10, 1935.
29 July 3, 1935.

"*Dirty linen*" device

The indispensable supplement to innuendo is actual or imaginary revelation. Thomas often made "if you only knew" promises in his radio speeches and then actually told the story in his church. Once more, the relation of the trick to commercial advertising is obvious. People are allowed to peep behind the scene, as it were, and to learn the inside story. They seem to share the privilege of the well-informed few. This idea is reminiscent of the "ingroup" aspect mentioned above.

In order to grasp the deeper psychological implications of this device, one must look at the peculiar contents to which propagandistic revelations usually refer. They belong, in most cases, to the sphere of scandal-mongering and usually pertain either to graft and corruption, or to sex.

One might well compare the psychological mechanism set in motion by the "dirty linen" device to a certain gesture which one can observe in many people. When they smell a bad odor, they very often do not turn away but eagerly breathe the pested air, sniff the stench and pretend to identify it while complaining of its repulsiveness. One does not have to be a psychoanalyst to suspect that these people unconsciously enjoy the bad smell. The appeal of scandal stories is very similar. Indignation about a scandal is in most cases a thin rationalization; actually the listener finds some pleasure in the story. One may well assume that the dark, forbidden things whose revelation he indignantly enjoys are the same things that he himself would love to indulge in.

This mechanism has become automatized to such an extent that the gratification comes to be derived from the act of revelation as such, no matter what actually is revealed. Revelation *per se* is experienced as the fulfillment of a promise and obtains an almost ceremonial character which may be colored by religious memories.

This accounts for one of the strangest phenomena concerned in the "dirty linen" device: the striking disproportion between the objective weight of the revealed facts, and the psychological importance they gain. The fascist-minded listener, at least, is willing to accept without examination any scandal story, even a most stupid one like the ritual murder legend. Furthermore, he generalizes cases which may happen under any political system, regarding them as typical of democracy, especially of its "plutocratic" nature. He becomes furious about facts which at closer scrutiny appear most innocent, or belong so strictly to the sphere of private life that nobody has a moral right to interfere. Thus, a certain fur coat of the Berlin *Bürgermeister,* supposedly a bribe, played a tremendous role in Nazi propaganda during the last years of the Weimar Republic, although the possession of a fur coat could not possibly be regarded as an outrageous luxury. What mattered was the revelation, not the fact.

Generally, the scandals which are revealed are quite unspecific and by no means characterize only those who are vilified. Thus, the Nazis made the most of certain corruption cases in which Jews – the Barmats, Kutisker, and the Sklareks – were involved. During the same period, and due to the same economic conditions, there were even bigger corruption cases on the right – the Lahusen case and the Neudeck affair which amounted to bribery of the *Reichspräsident* Hindenburg himself. These latter cases, however, were quickly oppressed and got little publicity. This may partly be explained by the fact that reaction controlled most public communications during the later years of the Weimar Republic. In general, there seems to be a greater indulgence in the airing of dirty linen among reactionaries than among progressives. The shift of social problems to private responsibilities, a general mood of repressiveness which tends to blacken anyone who enjoys himself rather than proves his acquisitive efficiency, and shrewd speculation on certain instincts of the frustrated majority may account for this fact. Those who want conditions to be unchanged are always ready to put the blame for any evil upon individuals who do not comply with the accepted standards of morality. Hypocrisy is a prerogative of conformism.

It is not absent from Thomas' arsenal. In his case, however, the simple motive of gratification to be obtained through spicy revelations overshadows most other considerations. Though he particularly relishes picturing the Communists as a lot of wanton criminals, it does not matter too much to him whether the scandals he divulges affect friend or foe. He occasionally describes himself as a victim of scandal stories.

I will never forget that, my first experience as a pastor in San Pedro and a situation I found myself in, when I arrived and I got into a terrific feud over a moral issue. A scandal sheet appeared about me that was my first experience with morale ... they used a criminal who professed conversion, but he had been sent in there by these people to gather information and blacken my name and they published all the things in the world that they could think about me, but within the flight of twelve months, I found out what it was. I found that a man who was really of the underworld of this city had been paying for that. I thank God through every conflict in my life that I have gone through, my Lord and Savior has stood by me.[30]

Curiosity aroused by reference to the sheet is compensated by the scandal stories that Thomas tells about others. The most outstanding is one about a phony decree concerning the general prostitution of womanhood in Russia. In his own church, he went into juicy details, in true Streicher style. In his radio addresses, he soft-pedals the story and relies on innuendo as being perhaps even more effective than revelation:

That contains the startling decree of Moscow concerning the making free of womanhood in Russia. Let me read just for a moment, my friend, in connection with that, the word of an outstanding woman, the wife of an American engineer, Mrs. McMurray, who came back just a few months ago. She said about Russia, 'I will never go back.' She said, 'sorrow and fear and hate combined with the jeering contempt for the finer things of life hang over the land of the Soviet.' Then she declared, 'no moral code is preserved. Men and women live together like animals. They live where and how the government directs. All labor is forced. If they do not work where the government commands, they are refused food-cards. I could not make friends. People are afraid of everyone and everything. Such is the red paradise.'[31]

It should be noted that this quotation, introduced by Thomas "in connection with" the supposed prostitution of woman-

30 July 1, 1935.
31 July 7, 1935.

hood in Russia, contains no specific reference to such prostitution but only a vague complaint about men and women living together "like animals." Thus the quotation sounds like a kind of anticlimax. But emphasis is laid upon the act of revelation as such. Through the "dirty linen" device, propaganda itself becomes the purpose of propaganda.

Be certain to get your request in quickly for the new edition of the *Christian American Crusader.* This will contain information of the Communists' and radicals' attack upon the clergy of America. The plots of the Communists are almost impossible to believe. I am giving you the whole setup. I am giving the names as I did Sunday night. By the way, I am giving more of this next Sunday night.[32]

"Tingling backbone" device

The "dirty linen" device is universally bound up with the tendency to terrorize listeners. When they are told that womanhood is prostituted in Russia they are made to fear that the same will happen to their wives, sisters, and daughters. Communist atrocities disclosed to them become threats of what will happen to themselves tomorrow. Here the double and almost self-contradictory character of the device is outspoken. The surface effect is that people react, out of fear, by organizing themselves to combat the threatening danger. The unconscious effect is, bluntly speaking, that they enjoy the description of atrocities because they themselves want to commit them some day. Pleasure in cruelty is closely related to pleasure in filth.

Fortunately, Thomas himself was kind enough to formulate a sentence which so plainly exhibits ambivalence towards atrocity stories that our interpretation can hardly be regarded as a matter of arbitrary speculation: "You also, send for the 'Imminent Peril of Communism for This Nation,' and after you read that, if your backbone does not tingle, then, my friend, there is something wrong with you."[33]

32 July 9, 1935.
33 July 7, 1935.

The promise to make the reader's backbone tingle has sense only if the sensation in store for the reader is in some respect pleasant to him. Thomas does not even care to hide this.

One aspect of propaganda through terror ought to be stressed particularly. It is generally assumed that fascist agitators promise everything to everyone. Scrutiny of Thomas' speeches at least makes the validity of this hypothesis rather doubtful. Thomas actually promises very little – mostly rewards in Eternity. Instead he terrorizes his audience by constantly pointing out all sorts of threats to them. He does not rely so much on their desire for happiness as on their fear that things may become even worse, while ceaselessly stressing that they are desperate even now. Rationally this evokes the worries of small people – the loss of their property and security. But this rational or half-rational stimulus is probably not the decisive one. The promise implied in terror propaganda is rather that of destruction as such. This leads to a certain quali-fication of our thesis on ambivalence. It would be perhaps too rationalistic to assume that the atrocities are necessarily those one wants to commit against the weak, though doubtlessly this impulse plays a major role. But the masochistic component is no less developed than the sadistic one. The prospective fascist may long for the destruction of himself no less than for that of the adversaries, destruction being a substitute for his deepest and most inhibited desires. This is confirmed by the constant references of fascists to self-sacrifice, or by certain statements made by Hitler, such as the one referred to by Rauschning, that if Hitler looses a *Ragnarök,* a Twilight of the Gods will take place. Here the fascist's subconscious know-ledge of the ultimate hopelessness of his undertakings proba-bly comes into play. He realizes that his solution is no solution, that in the long run it is doomed. Any keen observer could notice this feeling in Nazi Germany before the war broke out. Hopelessness seeks a desperate way out. Annihilation is the psychological substitute for the millenium – a day when the difference between the ego and the others, between poor and rich, between powerful and impotent, will be submerged in one great inarticulate unity. If no hope of true solidarity is held out to the masses, they may desperately stick to this negative substitute.[34]

Thomas' call to follow him as leader is terroristic. His followers are told that they should believe, without a clear distinction as to whether they are to believe in God or in Thomas. But those who do not believe are going to be punished anyway:

Now, remember that with belief you may do it. Isn't it worth while? I say that you must do it. You must accept Jesus Christ, the Son of the living God as your personal Savior from the penalty of power of indwelling sin. Now, unless you do that, you are a lost man or a lost woman. You are not only lost in this life but your soul shall be lost in that world which is to come. I have been praying lately that God would give me the true conception of a lost soul (!) and I am not sure that I have it, this morning, and I am not sure that you have it, this morning, for if I believe this word as I should believe it, I want to tell you that I would be crying to God night and day.[35]

The prayer for the true conception of a lost soul is an involuntary hint of the gratification he gets out of the lurid. Instead of praying that the lost soul may be saved he wishes to give as vivid a picture of the "lost" as possible. The associational sequence of his ideas converts this picture into a means of terrorizing his audience. He wants them to cry to God night and day. He expects that readiness to follow him may spring out of their fear as well as out of their masochistic pleasure in the imagery of the lost soul. It is hardly accidental that this attempt to terrorize the audience is linked up with the concept of belief. People are terrorized in order to believe, to wit, to

34 The tendency towards general destruction is particularly marked in Germany, both because of certain traditions of the German situation in terms of world competition. The feeling of this hopelessness has never subsided under the Hitler regime. Yet this general destructiveness is by no means totally absent from the American scene. We call to mind here only the affair of Orson Welles' "Invasion from Mars," and the success of the San Francisco picture which relishes the details of a blind natural catastrophe. This destructiveness is directed first against civilization as such. Only afterwards it is mobilized against certain groups, such as the Negroes or the Jews. (Cf. Hadley Cantril, *The Invasion from Mars* [Princeton: Princeton University Press, 1940].)

35 May 25, 1935.

stop thinking. Conversely, terrorized people are incapable
of clear thinking and are reduced to the blind reactions of the
sauve-qui-peut-pattern, an attitude particularly favorable to
adherence to a leader who promises to think and act for them
if only they trust in him. In order to achieve this, Thomas
skillfully confuses the threat of eternal penalties with the threat
of earthly unpleasantness, and makes metaphysical salvation
synonymous with membership in the Christian American
Crusade:

I appeal to the man who walks the streets that you remember there
is coming a day, my friends, when God will compel you to give an
account of the deeds that you are done in the body [*sic*]. My friend,
are you an American? Are you a Christian? If you are, you will take
cognizance of the situation facing America, but if you are not, you
are a coward.[36]

Since a Presbyterian clergyman cannot well threaten with
concentration camps he manipulates Eternity in such a way
that it serves exactly the same purpose. Thus the most modern
pattern of oppression by terror draws upon the oldest resource
of terrorism.

"Last hour" device

Another aspect of Thomas' terror technique ought to be
stressed. It consists of the direct or indirect assertion that a
catastrophe is imminent, that the situation is desperate and has
reached a peak of crisis, that some change must be made
immediately. "Thinking men and women across this nation
are fast going to their feet, for they know that things cannot
go on much longer as they are."[37] In Thomas' propaganda
every hour is the last hour.

One is reminded at first sight of the common pattern of advertising: "This offer holds good only for a few days." People are
admonished to act at once, to join the movement without
further delay. Behind this lies the simple consideration that

36 May 26, 1935.
37 July 14, 1935.

people tend to forget what they do not carry out right now. Particularly, terroristic stimuli, which always carry with themselves most unpleasant connotations, are likely to be psychologically repressed fairly soon. Terroristic propaganda works only "on the spot."

This, however, scratches only the surface of the phenomenon. The reference to impending doom, and particularly to an impending world catastrophe, is much older than industrial society. It has its roots in the apocalyptic element of Christian religion. It is not accidental that Thomas, like all revivalist sectarians, often refers to the biblical battle of Armageddon, which he skillfully confuses with the activities of his group.

Moreover, Thomas, in apparent contradiction to all the propagandistic devices implied by the "*fait accompli*" technique, often depicts his own organization as facing an immediate crisis, as being in desperate need of funds, and sometimes goes so far as to pretend that he cannot carry on forty-eight hours longer. His speeches constantly present every issue as a critical one calling for immediate action. There is a considerable gap between his passionate appeals to save the nation in the "last hour," and the comparatively weak and accidental indices of impending doom he provides – mostly complaints about the decrease of Christian orthodoxy or a spreading of atheistic teachings in the universities. A typical example of the mixture of insignificant complaints and apocalyptic diatribes is the following:

The lack of power and faithfulness in the ministries and the worldliness of the churches, the decrease of membership and the spirit of the Antichrist which is now spreading its great tentacles in our universities, and the undermining of our states, of our government, all point out to the certain serious crisis which at last has come upon us.[38]

"Serious crisis" has become a "magical word," and the existence of such a crisis is stressed at any price, even through such ludicrous statements as the decrease of church membership. Thomas presumes that his followers think in terms of their own narrowest experiences, and that their interest is centered

38 July 14, 1935.

around church matters. An empty church supposedly suffices to convince them of the imminent danger of a collapse of the American nation.

A tentative explanation of the irrational emphasis laid upon the idea of crisis may be the following: Thomas, like all fascists, reckons with followers who are deeply discontended and also even destitute. Their objective situation might possibly convert them into radical revolutionaries. One of the main tasks of the fascist is to prevent this and to divert revolutionary trends into their own line of thought, for their own purposes. In order to achieve this aim, the fascist agitator steals, as it were, the concept of revolution. Again, the idea of catastrophe, of the fateful moment, is the substitute. It implies radical change without, however, having any specific social contents. Nobody looks beyond the end of the world. Moreover, catastrophe is something that happens to people rather than materializing by their own free will. They are divested of their spontaneity and transformed into spectators of the great world-historical events which are going to be decided over their heads, while their own energies are absorbed by their adherence to the organization, and their love for the leader.

Psychoanalysis has sometimes noted that a neurotic feeling of impotence is often expressed through a peculiar attitude towards the element of *time*. The less one is capable of acting on one's own account, the more one is likely to expect everything from time *in abstracto*: "It cannot go on like this much longer." The "last hour" device feeds on this disposition. Time as such is made a guarantor of coming change and therefore the "follower" is rid of his own responsibility. He simply has to do what "the hour calls for." By presenting this hour as the *last* hour – "Communism is not coming, it is right here" – this device is linked to the "*fait accompli*" technique.

Of course, the catastrophe is described throughout Thomas' speeches not as something desirable but as a danger. But this is hardly more than a rationalization. Apart from an emotional emphasis laid upon the idea of catastrophe which seems to take it for granted that this notion is not altogether unwelcome to the listeners, there is an easy transition from warning of the danger of catastrophe to advertising it. If the situation is desperate, desperate means are necessary: The answer to the "imminent danger of Communism" is the eradication of Communists, radicals, and "those evil forces," that is, the pogrom. The idea that some change has to be made, abstract and yet with so many associations of violence and brutality, is the necessary consequence of the "last hour" device. The last hour of which the fascist warns is actually the putsch which he wants to commit himself. Purely negative punitive action substitutes for a rational policy by which things might really become better.

I believe I know some of the things you are going to do, because I know of the kind of material that is on the inside of those bodies of yours, I believe that you are going to seek the truth. I believe I know just how you are going to act. I believe that you are going to rise up in your wrath, in your indignation, in your love for the old flag, you are going to say to these forces that have taken our nation down to the very depths: thus far shalt thou go and not one step farther. Now, I believe you are going to do that.[39]

It is interesting to note that Thomas' clamor for an "awakening"[40] to the threat of the impending catastrophe is conceived in terms of "back" rather than of "forward." The awakening of America is represented as a restoration of something long over. Moreover, it is understood as an act not of conscious self-determination, but of bowing to the authority of the father. In fact, it is just the opposite of what one should expect such an awakening to be: "Awake, America, back to your knees, back to the father of the fathers, to the place where God would have you to be."[41] Here Thomas comes unwittingly near to one of the favorite concepts of fascist and anti-Semitic intellectuals, that nonentity, the "conservative revolution."

39 June 4, 1935.
40 Cf. "indefatigability" device.
41 July 13, 1935.

"Black hand" (Feme) *device*

It has been noted above that the "innuendo" technique is related to the idea of a closed, violent, strictly ruled ingroup – a racket. This relationship makes itself keenly felt in the terror propaganda of fascism. Strongly reminiscent of plain, non-political racketeering, terror is applied no less, and perhaps even more, to one's own followers than to the opponents. This technique played a very large role in Nazidom under the title of *"Feme."* The most dangerous forces are supposedly those working from inside. The Fascist cannot help feeling surrounded by traitors, and so continuously threatens to exterminate them.

By innuendo Thomas calls for the universal vigilance of one "crusader" against the other:

My friend, I am never afraid of the world. I am never fearful of the attack of Satan. I know where to place the world. I know where to place those who are on the other side, but I tell you, my friend, you must be careful within. Some one will get on the inside of the church and yield himself to the Devil and attempt to kill the work of God by somebody inside the church. I have never been attacked in the years, except it has come from within. You men and women will always bear me witness of that fact. You look out for the attack within with some one very close to you, through jealousy or some other thing, that Satan will bring upon them.[42]

Often enough the fascist leader has actual reasons for such warnings. Rackets attract racketeers; criminals are prone to join all sorts of hooligan organizations and they are likely, for various reasons, to quit and go over to any other party from whom they expect more. Furthermore, the element of secrecy inherent in all kinds of fascist conspiracies breeds indiscretion and treachery. Terror, directed against the insiders, strengthens the authority which appears to be absolute only if no infringement whatsoever is tolerated, if the strictest discipline is enforced. This can be achieved only if even the slightest deviation is branded as treachery, and ruthlessly persecuted.

But here, again, certain deeper-lying issues enter the picture. The "black hand" device is a complement of the "unity"

42 July 13, 1935.

trick, a means of integrating the divergent elements of a repressive and exclusive organization. Its exclusiveness can be maintained only by vigilantism, by spying among the members who are kept in a permanent state of mutual distrust. The *"Feme"* threat which the fascist agitator utters against his own followers foreshadow the complete atomization of the whole population which takes place in totalitarian states. Repressive unity results in the oppression of all non-professional activities not immediately controlled by the government, or the party. Conspirators must be kept completely alienated from each other with regard to their convictions if they are to form a compact group. The fascist racket is the very parody of that *"Volksgemeinschaft,"* people's community, that it boasts of being. Fellow members of fascist organizations are more jealous, more suspicious, more ready to "liquidate" each other than even the most hard-boiled competitors. To point this out would be the real answer to the "human interest" trick.

However, the most sinister implication of the "black hand" device pertains to one of the innermost characteristics of racketeering and fascism. Both may be defined as types of organizations *from which there is no way back.* The sacrifice of the individual to the collectivity discussed above means that one has to surrender totally, with soul and body, without qualification or reservation. This is expressed by the postulate of irrevocability, by oaths, blood symbolism, initiation rites, etc. The wish to "get out" of a compulsory community is the primary gesture by which the longing for freedom expresses itself. Nothing is more hideous to the fascist than this desire. He who changes his mind and who wants to "get out again," no matter what his motives may be or how essentially decent he may be, is regarded as the arch-enemy. Hence, change of opinion as such is characterized as treachery, and put under severe punishment. As important as the organizatory effect of the *"Feme"* idea is the psychological one: whoever enters the organization is made to understand that there is no way out, and the character of irrevocability thus bestowed upon his decision works only as an emotional tie to the racket. The effect is by no means only fear. People tend to love that which they cannot quit – to identify themselves with even their prison walls. It is this particular disposition on which the fascist emphasis upon "*Feme*" persistently feeds.

The most blatant example of the "black hand" device took place on June 30, 1934, with the shooting of a large number of Nazis, some of whom may not have been conspirators at all, with due consideration to the propagandistic effect. Thomas' mentality shows perhaps unwitting traces of an attitude which finally develops into the pitiless terrorization of one's own organization. This ultimate twisting of terror toward just the "ingroup" should be stressed by counterpropaganda.

"*Let us be practical*"

Hitler, following Bismarckian tradition, often speaks about *Realpolitik*. In his case, this simply refers to the right of the strong. However, the term has deeper implications than a mere rationalization of Machiavellian cynicism. In spite of the perennial appeal to idealism, heroism, and the spirit of sacrifice, the fascist never forgets to keep his followers aware that, essentially, he does not want the evil to disappear from the world. He aims at his own group's taking over the reins, but not at an abolition of repression itself. He derides any idea of "Utopia" and enjoys the notion that the world is not only bad, but that it shall remain essentially as bad as it is, and that it is a punishable crime to think that it could be essentially different. This device has worked with all reactionary theoreticians since Hobbes, and has followed like a shadow all the high-sounding ideologies of the modern age. In a completely deteriorated form which, however, sheds light upon the ultimate content of this idea, it recurs in Thomas. Whereas he preaches lofty religious ideals, most of them smelling of such an outdated orthodoxy that he cannot seriously expect his followers to be convinced, he also shows a passionate interest in all sorts of practical matters, of *Realpolitik* in the pettiest sense of the word. He displays a rationalism in calculating and organizing his group which conflicts at every point with the sturdy irrationality of his religious teachings. It is the distance of his "practical" common-sense passages from his official ideology, which demonstrates, to the subconscious at least, the impotence of those ideals themselves and their ultimate spuriousness. The ideals serve mainly to veil superficially his lust for power and his administrative manipulation, and to brand the adversaries as being morally inferior. The practical down-to-earth passages, however, show to the audience not only that their leader is a man of common sense as they think they are, but also that what actually matters to them is an organization, competitive power, and an earthly success. It is hard to say whether the blatant contradiction between high-flown phraseology and down-to-earthness is entirely conscious with Thomas, or whether it is due to his actually representing an average lower-middle-class type. But however this may be, this contradiction is not so much an obstacle to the effectiveness of his speeches as an auxiliary force in making them effective. The less interconnected the ideal and, as he sometimes chooses to call it, his "business" are, the more distinctly the audience realizes that the ideals are ideals, but that he means business.

One could not formulate the configuration between the apparently irreconcilable elements of Thomas' speeches more clearly than he himself does: "We try to be practical here. We try to preach the gospel of our Lord within all of the fervor, and the love, and the power that God gives us through the spirit."[43]

The idea of being practical refers above all to money, to the money he wants to obtain as well as to the money of his followers. God the Almighty and the printer's bill are indiscriminately lumped together:

We have a mighty God. If we honor him, he will take care of every need. We have got to pay bills today – this radio, printer's bill, office help, telephone. Listen, get down and help us. I am not asking you to do anything that I am not doing. My family are sacrificing every possible dollar that we can, because we want to see this movement going across the United States. I find many people of many sections are listening and praying and blessing God.[44]

43 June 9, 1935.
44 May 27, 1935.

The idea that God takes care of every need is interpreted by Thomas even more practically: he regards God as a sort of investment consultant.

Go and sin no more. A great many people have lost material possession. They have lost stocks and bonds and various things. I want to say to you, today, that no man or woman has ever consulted God about any investment and has listened to God, alone, and lost. If you go to God and lay it before the Lord, you have never lost a dollar, but if you have not, you fail at once.[45]

The implication, again, builds a sort of mild blackmail. To be faithful to God is as much as "being faithful with the tithes of God"[46] and the tithes of God are always liberally interpreted by Thomas as the donation to "this movement."

The patriotic ideal fares no better than the religious one. The appeal to save America is confused with the fear that the stocks may lose their value. It is strongly suggested by Thomas that the great fight against the Antichrist is a practical one, namely that it serves to safeguard one's private property, as "those evil forces" want to take away the property of the small man.

Ah, my friend, will you help us to meet God's little children before the Antichrist comes, before the wolves of life could possibly take them and tear them to pieces. You see, well, I am being satisfied as a whole. Why should I worry? My friend, listen, when the Antichrist takes hold of America, and he will take hold in the very immediate near future unless you and I and millions like us are able to hold back those forces for a little while longer, that [sic] your stocks will be useless, that [sic] your home will be of no use. My dear brother, my dear sister, it is now or never. You cannot, my friend, afford not to have a part in this great Christian American program. You cannot afford to have this message of God go off this radio for the lack of your support.[47]

The practical spirit (monetary categories) is applied even to Biblical stories such as, of all things, that of Mary Magdalen sacrificing to Christ:

There were men in that day, as well as in this day, who made a business of collecting that pure oil, a little drop of which would so odorize a room that the scent of it would last for hours. She saw

45 June 5, 1935.
46 *Ibid.*
47 July 5, 1935.

what was coming. Like the woman that she was, she prepared for it. She saved up her dimes and nickels. Now, what do you suppose, even in that day, it cost her to collect that whole . . . , about 300 shillings, a shilling being about 17 cents now, 300 times 17 and you will have the amount there, about $51. You multiply the purchasing power in that day with this day, perhaps a hundred times the purchasing value, and you will secure some general idea of the cost to Mary. It may well have been that Mary sacrificed, sacrificed all her possessions, indeed. It is my opinion that she did. She went and sold, she perhaps sold her house and let . . . .[48]

The implications of this passage are manifold. There is, first of all, the old exegetic technique of translating Biblical stories into terms of the everyday life of the listeners in order to make it more understandable to them – hence, the dimes and nickels. But this is merely the surface. The listener is actually conveyed the idea that even the most sublime actions of the Bible are "practical," that they can be expressed, as it were, in money, and that money is the measurement for everything, even for religious ecstasy, so that indirectly the most earthly concepts become a yardstick for the supposedly sublime ones. While apparently the magnitude of Mary's sacrifice is exalted, it is, in a deeper psychological sense, divested of its dignity and made profane by its transformation into dollars and purchasing value; and the crusader is made to realize that it is these which count, and not religion which has to be translated into them in order to make any sense at all. One may safely assume that there are few devices employed in Thomas' technique which meet with a greater response from his audience than this poor one. Indeed, his speeches are larded with intentionally trite, mundane, practical passages of which the preceding ones are but a few examples gathered at random.

One may well object that we have made more of this particular device than there is to it. It may be understood as a simple appeal to the traditional, practical sense of the Americans which cannot be reached by any ideals unless they are put immediately into "operational terms." One may even point to homiletic traditions in American sects and in institutions such as the Salvation Army or Christian Science, where religion is

48 July 12, 1935.

transformed into something utterly pragmatic in order that it
may be at all acceptable to the American people. Even if this
is to be admitted, one can hardly deny that the trick of
"pragmatism" in apparently idealistic issues has obtained a
new meaning. Formerly, it may have been a means to the end
of religious conversion and more or less genuine revivals.
Today for fascist propaganda, revivals and conversions have
become a means to the end that people might become practical,
that is to say that they might yield any theoretical thought of
their own, might become integrated into teams and organizations, and might take action in accordance with their collective
interest rather than with their rational conviction. The lack of
capacity for abstraction, the old compulsion to "illustrate"
any concept by its most immediate application which often
implies a deterioration of its true meaning, this incapacity for
abstraction which is more likely to have become stronger than
to have decreased under modern conditions, is used as a lever
for propagandistic purposes. The ideal that becomes immediately and inconsiderately identified with some practical measure
or attitude, becomes meaningless as an ideal and is reduced to
a mere embellishment of the next practical step. This, however is actually what Thomas' propaganda, like that of all
fascists, aims at. Conscience becomes nothing but an ideology
which lends its glamour to the deeds of naked self-interest,
carried out by the organization. By discrediting the ideas while
they are being transformed into terms of practical, everyday
life, the follower is made to understand that what matters
is not the idea, not even the intentionally vague "matter for
which it stands," but in the last analysis only the organization
itself, that is to say, the power apparatus and that authority
which finally decides what policy is expedient.

SECTION III:
The Religious Medium

Introductory Remarks

Thomas' racket is religion. It provides the characteristic color of his speeches, the trademark by which he can be distinguished from competitors. As a minister, he can appear as an expert promoting the specific interests of a specific group. The basic idea of the whole framework is to appeal to people of orthodox and even bigoted religious leanings, mainly Protestant fundamentalists, and to transform their religious zeal into political partisanship and subservience. It is this transformation rather than the more or less obsolescent religious doctrines of Thomas which make it worthwhile to consider his theological manipulations. In Germany, religion played but a minor role in fascist propaganda, and it is a well known fact (though probably an overrated one in its actual importance) that fascism took a definite stand against practicing Protestants, as well as against Catholics. At any rate, the whole Nazi tradition is bound up with a certain tradition of monistic "free thinking" which in many respects is actually hostile to Christianity. Its belief in the unbridled and blind forces of nature, concomitant with the expansion of German imperialism, is the source of a decisive difference between the American and the German scene. American fascist propaganda shows a very strong affinity to certain religious movements, a fact that is testified by the major role played in fascist propaganda here by clergymen of various denominations.[1]

The pragmatic value of a survey of some of the more specific characteristic aspects of Thomas' theology lies, above all, in the possibility of making clear the background of his

1 Such as, for instance, [Gerald B.] Winrod, Coughlin, Jeffers, and Hubbard.

psychological technique. Many of the "devices" so far discussed consist of secularizations of religious stimuli which he
expects still to operate within his listeners. The *"fait accompli"*
technique is reminiscent of the Protestant doctrine of predesti-
nation; the "last hour" device, of the apocalyptic mood of
certain sects; the dogmatic dichotomy between "those evil
forces" and "the forces of God," of Christian dualism; the
exaltation of the humble folk, of the Sermon on the Mount,
etc. Without this associational background and the considerable weight of authority carried with it, his whole propagandistic setup probably would not have been half as
effective as it proved to be. It is therefore imperative to deal
explicitly with the theological elements of the propaganda of
Thomas and his ilk.

Fascist propaganda, by "secularizing" Christian motives, perverts a great many of them into their opposite. It is this
process with which we are mainly concerned here. We shall try
to bring out the contradiction between the religious stimuli
applied by Thomas and his ultimate aims. His true purposes
are, as we shall point out, antireligious. Thomas, the shrewd
mass-psychologist, knows why he talks religion: he must reckon
with the existence of religious feelings within his audience. If
the groups which he specifically addresses were shown unambig-
uously that his aims plainly contradict the Christian ideals
which he professes to uphold, these religious feelings might
express themselves in the opposite direction, just as they did in
Germany after the Nazis had shown their hand.

One qualification ought to be added. The use of religion for
fascist purposes and the perversion of religion into an instrument of hate-propaganda, though providing the principal
appeal, the trademark of Thomas, is by no means a unique
phenomenon. Innumerable spiritual trends within our existing
society point towards the establishment of some sort of
totalitarian regime. There can be little doubt that every shade
of prefascist ideology, be it religion or free-thinking, nationalism or pacifism, elite theories or folk ideologies, would be
swallowed by the totalitarian stream which is little troubled
by inconsistencies. Fascist rationality consists in the establish-

ment of an omnipotent power system rather than in the enforcement of any "philosophy." Thus, the importance of the dogmatic content of the religious medium as such must not be overrated. However, it is worth studying how such a concrete medium, apparently quite separate from fascist doctrine, is transformed to fit totalitarian purposes. Fascism could not possibly succeed without creeping into all the different and divergent forms of life. Thus, it has been effective in Germany with the Youth Movement and elderly homeowners, with bankrupt peasants and oversized industrial combines, with jobless, adventurous army officers and pedantic civil servants. The full comprehension of the magnetic power of totalitarianism necessitates an understanding of each of these aspects in its actual, concrete form.

One more reason for devoting attention to the religious medium of Thomas' propaganda should be mentioned. It is our assumption that the specific phenomenon of modern anti-Semitism is much more deeply rooted in Christianity than it would appear. It is true that the typical anti-Semite of our day, the highly rational, merciless, cynical, planning fascist, has as little belief in Christ as in anything else, except power. But it is no less true that the anti-Semitic ideas which form the spearhead of fascism everywhere could not possibly exercise such a strong appeal unless they had their strong sources, not only apart from, but also actually within Christian civilization. It would be difficult to exaggerate the role played by imagery of the Christ-killers, of the Pharisee, of the money-changers in the temple, of the Jew who forfeited his salvation by denying the Lord and not accepting Baptism. In another study, we shall try to point out the ultimate theological reasons for anti-Semitism, and their place in society and history.[2] Here we shall attempt to show these motives "in operation." A survey of Thomas' theological tricks may reveal the specific, though partly unconscious historical memories which an anti-Semitic agitator calls back to life. Long-term

2 Cf. Max Horkheimer and Theodor W. Adorno, "Elemente des Antisemitismus," *Dialektik der Aufklärung* (Amsterdam: Querido Verlag, 1947), pp. 199-244.

countermeasures should be directed against these memories, no
less than against obvious propaganda. Re-education should
bring to explicit consciousness the inherited theological imagery
of anti-Semitism and then cope with it. Only by cognition
and refutation may these clinging prejudices and also the
psychological mechanisms behind their obstinate survival be
rendered impotent.

"Speaking with tongues" device

Apart from any specific theological contents, and possibly
more effective propagandistically than any such contents, the
religious medium makes itself felt throughout the psychological atmosphere of Thomas' speeches. This atmosphere consists,
above all, of a certain unctuousness, a mixture of maudlin
sentimentality and phony dignity which tends to lend its own
aura to every sentence that he utters. Of course, this unctuousness may be attributed simply to Thomas' sermonizing
attitude. It ought to be noted, however, that Hitler himself,
who until recently very rarely referred to religion and then in
the most general terms, has developed a similar unctuousness
in speaking. The halo of "sacredness" has been emancipated
from any specific religious content. It is taken over by arbi-
trarily chosen concepts, mostly of an animistic connotation,
such as the ancestors, or the "dead of the movement." This
transfer is expressed in a general sentimentality of tone. This
sentimentality, its blatant insincerity and phonyness, makes it
most difficult for any intellectual to understand the effectiveness of fascist agitators. One should think, so runs the argument, that the simple people, with their feeling for the genuine,
would be repulsed by tones which are reminiscent of the wolf
in sheep's clothing. This assumption, however, is untrue.
Anyone familiar with folk art will find, particularly among
folk singers and folk actors, a very strong tendency toward
exaggerated sentimentality and "false tones." This can be
accounted for in part by the people's desire for "strong
colors" which, in a way, calls for overdoing things. But there is

a much deeper-lying basis, namely the longing of the people for "feigning" things. It is this attitude which regards an actor primarily as a man who can "pretend" well, can disguise himself, and impersonate others. People expect a "performance" rather than the presentation of the "genuine." They probably derive actual enjoyment from the false tones, because they regard them as indices of a "performance," of imitations of some model, no matter whether the model itself is known to them or not. This probably can be explained by the complex of "oppressed mimesis" discussed in other sections of our project.[3] The technique of false tones is particularly evident in the records of Thomas' speeches, but it sometimes can be spotted even in the typed material. Typical are passages such as the following which uses the tone of the *Kapuzinerpredigt*:

I compare this great nation of ours, what she has been yonder through the years and what she is at the present hour and of the future and of the change which she is now undergoing, I compare her past with her present, and then I compare womanhood, the home, and the church. Great tears run down my face as I think of what my nation has been, can be.[4]

Perhaps a realization of the audience's sense of "performance" also accounts at least partly for the hundreds and hundreds of pages full of the purest nonsense which one can find in Thomas' and, it may be added, in Hitler's uncensored speeches. Here again, personal shortcomings fit marvelously with public demands. It is indeed possible that an orator like Thomas with an hysterical character structure and a complete lack of intellectual inhibitions is actually incapable of building up a logical and meaningful sequence of statements. However, it is probably just this uninhibited ability to speak without thinking, a capacity traditionally associated with certain types of salesmen and carnival barkers, which fulfills a desire of the audience. Here comes into play the ambivalent admiration of people who are repressed and psychologically "mute" for those who can speak. The Jews are blamed for being glib, but the anti-Semitic agitator and his

[3 Cf. Horkheimer and Adorno, *Dialektik der Aufklärung*, passim.]
4 June 27, 1935.

audience long for this glibness and expect, in a way, that the
anti-Semitic agitator can "speak like a Jew." The ability to
chatter is taken as proof of a mysterious gift of speech. Thus,
the nonsense contained in all fascist speeches is not so much an
obstacle as a stimulant in itself. It also serves to underscore
the "dynamics" rather than any specific purposes of program.
The dynamics of unrestrained rhetoric are perceived as an
image of the dynamics of real events.

Maudlin ecstacy and senseless chatter, "to speak with tongues,"
points strongly in the direction of evangelism and revivalism,
which we shall discuss later in other respects. It is to this
tradition, genuine or artificial, that Thomas refers, and from
which he borrows the pattern of his general emotional religious
attitude:

Oh, brothers, let us seek the holy God and the blessings of the holy
God. If we will do that, our nation will be saved. If we will do
that, the church will have a mighty revival of God whereby any
day the people would see the holiness of God.[5]

He hopes that the grand days of revivalism will come back
under the impact of his political "crusade":

Is it any wonder that Communism has come in, that it takes hold of
our homes? Where are the men that should be raising the banners?
Where are the old leaders of the past? Why is it that we have not
great evangelical revivals? When you think of the days of Alexan-
der Moody, Billy Sunday, what has become of the evangelical fires
in America?[6]

Detailed study of the literature on revivalism, such as the
very revealing biography of Billy Sunday,[7] would yield
a great many of the psychological devices of modern fascist
propaganda, particularly those which consider the "fight
against the devil" as a kind of public performance, and those
which aim at a mimetic relationship between the preacher and
his audience.

5 July 10, 1935.
6 July 2, 1935.
[7 William Thomas Ellis, *Billy Sunday: The Man and His Message* (Phila-
delphia: The John C. Winston Company, 1936).]

"Decomposition" (Zersetzung) *device*

In order to modify religious contents for mundane, political purposes, they must be "neutralized." No matter how deeply religious bigotry is related to reactionary social trends such as anti-Semitism, the content of religion must undergo certain changes in order to be brought "down to earth." The modern fascist agitator reckons with religious motives only as atomized carry-overs of past religion; he assumes that any consistent belief has been shattered. He surveys the debris of traditional religion, selects what suits his purposes, and eliminates all the rest. In spite of his bigoted phraseology, he approaches religion in a thoroughly pragmatic manner. He takes no definite religious stand – a shortcoming for which he tries to compensate by claiming a position above dogmatic disputes, and by advocating religious unity. His theology is consistent only in one respect: antiliberalism. Religious antiliberalism cloaks the political antiliberalism which he dares not advocate openly, just as religious authority functions psychologically as a substitute for the political authoritarianism to come. Within the framework of general antiliberalism, however, Thomas draws upon orthodoxy – in particular, Southern fundamentalism – as well as upon evangelism and revivalism. This theological attitude is furthered by the fact that these trends have many likenesses, since both are "positive" in contrast to enlightened religion ("modernism") in this country. Thomas' nondiscriminatory attitude and his neutralization of religious teachings go so far, however, that he does not make the slightest objection to blatant contradictions between the religious trends he exploits. He sometimes poses as a defender of the Church, appears to identify himself with certain denominations, and rallies his "crusaders" with the battle cry: the Church is in danger. But sometimes he professes extreme religious subjectivism and goes so far as to state that the time of denominations is over – apparently with an eye to some future religious "integration" consummated by a totalitarian state. Of fundamentalism there is left little but the authoritarian claims as such, of secretarianism nothing but a rebellious gesture of hatred against established

institutions, state and Church, an attitude which paves the way
for fascist organization. This neutralization defines the framework of Thomas' manipulation of Protestantism.

In accordance with Thomas' general principle of evoking an
"against" rather than a "pro" attitude, the sectarian motive is
preponderant. But since in this country sects are traditional
powers themselves, and the sectarian outlook is basic for the
whole religious approach, his sectarianism, too, is capable of
traditionalist, orthodox pretentions. It may very well be that
the vestiges of religious authority and live religious feelings
on which Thomas relies are due to the essentially "sectarian"
character of religion in America, in contrast to the established
churches in Germany which were more or less state institutions.
American sects, being closer, as it were, to the individual's
personal beliefs, emotions and traditional particularities,
have a stronger hold over the individual than they do in
Germany. The American idea was to choose a religion of one's
own, rather than to conform to a given one. This produces a
much more intimate relationship between the individual and
his religious behaviour patterns, even now when the dogmatic
differences between the sects play but a minor role. The
organizational hold of the sect over the family, its appeal to
tradition, is much stronger than in Germany, where at least
the Protestant Church has been reduced for centuries to a
kind of "social function." The fascist agitator has to reckon
with the presence of sectarian substance within the individual,
secularized though the form may be. An agitator cannot simply
oppose this substance; he must try to lead it into the channels
of his own purposes. This, however, is not too difficult. Some
of the more radical sects have developed within their own
womb certain traces of repressiveness and even – under the
name of apocalyptic trends – destructiveness. Thus they show
a more real affinity to fascism than the big European denominations ever did. Moreover, the nucleus of all fascist movements was always somewhat like a sect, with all the features
of intolerance, exclusiveness, and particularism. It is this deep-
rooted similarity between the political and the religious sect
upon which fascist propaganda in this country feeds.

This general "sectarian" background paradoxically accounts for the virility of certain "orthodox" stimuli. There is, for example, an ecclesiastical model for the "desperate" situation which fascist propaganda always constructs. In Thomas, it is expressed in the complaint about the threatening disintegration of Christianity because of the spirit of rationalism. It is this negative aspect, this supposed danger of decomposition, which reveals Thomas' affinity to fundamentalism. According to Thomas the Church, interpreted as a kind of microcosm of the nation, is in dire jeopardy. The impending triumph of the devil in Communism, the "progressive spirit" of the established denominations, and the plots of "those evil forces," all make for this disintegration of the Church. The situation calls for an "integration" in the fascist sense.

Only during the past three years, according to the official Communist reports, they have enrolled between four and five million of our young people between the age of sixteen and thirty. They are pitting the growing youth of this nation against the Christian institutions, against the Church of the nation, against the Constitution.... Today, freedom of religion prevails everywhere; so it will be only a few years before Christianity will fall to pieces.[8]

The attack upon "freedom" within the Church, sounding definitely antisectarian, indicates clearly what is behind Thomas' phrases when he elsewhere professes to defend the liberties granted by the Constitution.

Thomas' fight against the supposed decomposition of traditional belief by religious modernism has a specific aspect. It is directed against the notion of progress and against biological materialism. Thomas apparently wanted to make friends with the fundamentalist Baptists, though his kind of propaganda suffered rebukes from official fundamentalism.

Here is a letter from the pastor of one of the Baptist churches here in California, a man that is doing an outstanding piece of work: "I have been very much impressed with two things, the imminent peril that confronts us and, second, with your Christian stand. I will stand shoulder to shoulder to put down modernism and Communism."

8 July 3, 1935.

I thank God for the word of this outstanding Christian minister that is back of us in our program.[9]

Thomas sympathizes with fundamentalism mainly because of its fight against the theory of evolution which represents to him the acme of subversive modernism.

Now, listen, there was a day when we believed that the Bible was the word of God, but today, we teach evolution and organic evolution. You know some educators used to laugh at William Jennings Bryan, but I want to tell you that Bryan was a prophet. William Jennings Bryan was a Christian ... Bryan attacked Darwinism. He attacked Nietzscheism. He attacked these things that he saw were undermining this nation of ours ..... William Jennings Bryan saw that in another generation or two, that unless the evolutionary teaching that we simply came from the ape family, that we were only the result, my friend, of coming up through the anthropoidae, if that thing continued in this country, this nation of ours will, with her institutions, is bound to go down.[10]

It is noteworthy that Thomas attacks Darwinism not because it is untrue, but because of its supposedly bad moral effect – for purely pragmatic reasons. He conceives the religious orthodoxy which he advocates purely as a means of keeping discipline. But this leads to strange inconsistencies. As will be shown later, Thomas unconsciously falls back into animism by attributing a theological meaning to natural events such as earthquakes. Yet he consciously becomes indignant as soon as he is made aware of man's kinship with nature. Nothing irks the neo-pagan barbarians more than the idea that their ancestors might have been apes. Counterpropaganda, in analyzing the implicit philosophy of the fascists, should carefully point out their twisted relationship to nature. They adore nature as far as nature expresses domination and terror, as it is symbolized by the earthquake. They abhor nature as far as it is concomitant with the undisciplined and childlike, in other words, with everything that is not "practical" in the sense discussed above. They favor the carnivorous, preying beast and despise the playful, harmless animal. They believe in the survival of the fittest, in natural selection, but hate the idea

9 May 25, 1935.
10 May 26, 1935.

that their antics may be reminiscent of those of the monkey. This inconsistency is an index of the whole fascist attitude.

"Sheep and bucks" device

Another morsel Thomas snatches from authoritarian orthodoxy is the violent condemnation of the sinner and the idea that the difference between sinner and just has been established once and for all. The sectarian, not to speak of the heretic, is always prone to think of the salvation of the sinner, either by conversion or by the mystical conception of sin itself as of the precondition of redemption. Conversely, orthodox, established religion has little use for the sinner, that is, for anyone who has not surrendered himself completely to institutionalized religion. The sinner is visualized as definitely condemned. This trend once was associated with the organizing power of the church. Thomas borrows it with his own organization in the back of his mind. His predilection for the role of infallible judge makes itself felt in the selections rather than in the nature of his theological concepts, which are without exception taken from the New Testament. Roughly speaking, all the reconciliatory features of Christian teaching, including the idea of *caritas*, are omitted. But there is constant stress on the negative elements, such as the idea of the evil and eternal punishment, the defamation of the intellect, and the exclusiveness of Christianity against other religions, particularly Judaism. His Biblical citations are preferably taken from the Gospel of St. John, partly because of his general apocalyptic and mystical mood, partly because that Gospel lends itself more easily to anti-Semitic maneuvers than do the synoptics.

This selective technique enhances theologically the "sheep and bucks" device. This device is stressed in many analyses of fascist propaganda, such as in the above mentioned Coughlin study[11] under the title of "Name calling" and "Card stacking." Hitler has pointed out in *Mein Kampf* that propaganda, in order to be effective, must always paint the adversary as

[11 Lee and Lee, *The Fine Art of Propaganda*, pp. 26-46; 95-104.]

the arch enemy and one's own group as invested with everything noble and admirable. With Thomas, this device obtains
a specific color by being tied up with religious dualism. He
assumes that a transcendent struggle between the Kingdom of
God and the realm of the Devil is taking place between the
political powers of our time. He admits no intermediary
processes or dialectics. This serves to brand the adversary as
being "condemned" *a priori,* without recourse to argument.
"What am I to believe? Believe that Christ vanquished the
devils."[12] This dichotomy is applied directly to the political
scene. The issue, he says, had already been decided in the New
Testament. "Now folks, the battle is on. The forces of God and
Americanism on one side, and the forces of darkness and
Communism on the other."[13]

The devil is coming down and working through men and institutions
as never in the history of the world. Wherever you look, today, you
see the dark clouds that are coming. Wherever you look, today, you
see the prophetic Antichrist. At the present hour, there are millions
and millions of men and women yonder in the dark land of Russia
who are living under the control of the view of the Antichrist. My
friend, God makes it very clear.[14]

The theological dualism is used to invest the political fight,
in which Thomas is involved, with the dignity of a conflict
taking place within the absolute. No proof is given that the
Communists are devils or that Thomas is the partisan of God,
except that he carries God's name in his mouth. He simply
relies on the distinction of in- and outgroup. People he "takes
in" are good, and the others are sons of the Devil. Any argumentation would only weaken this mechanism. Incidentally,
his whole derogatory terminology, his allusion to "those evil
forces" and so forth is borrowed from the language of theological dualism. Every penny that he gets for his crusade is
transfigured into "ammunition" for the battle of Armageddon.

One peculiar aspect of the "sheep and bucks" device ought to
be mentioned. Of course Thomas, clinging to Christian concepts, refers to the forces of God in terms of inwardness, of

12 June 1, 1935.
13 June 12, 1935.
14 June 28, 1935.

moral grandeur rather than of physical strength. However, in his esoteric speeches, he cannot refrain from particularly applauding some "big boy" who has pledged his support. But here occurs a twist, exemplified by the following quotation: "They were playing upon the jealousy of John, but he was a big man, not physically, but he was big from the standpoint of spirit."[15] The notorious German Jew-baiter, Streicher, whose body is abnormally small, used exactly the same wording in interpretations of his idea of national-socialist greatness. One need not evoke an Adlerian psychology in order to find in such statements distinct traces of *Organminderwertigkeit,* a feeling of inferiority stemming from physical weakness. Thomas himself is quite a vigorous man, but he is a keen enough connoisseur of his listeners to manipulate this element of their psychology.

"Personal experience" device

The vague idea of a "conservative revolution," discussed in Section II, is rather concretely expressed in Thomas' theological ventures. We have seen that manipulated orthodoxy corresponds to the conservative authoritarian element. The quasi-revolutionary element is expressed by the revivalist, sectarian leaning of Thomas.

The non-conformism from which the American sects originally derived brought them into a certain opposition against centralized institutions such as "the Church" and "the state." This falls well in line with fascist ideology. The combination of an apparently rebellious or radical attitude, as in the sects, with authoritarian, ascetic, and repressive tendencies, parallels a familiar structure of the fascist mentality. National Socialism in particular has taken an "anti-state" attitude, and favors such concepts as the nation, the folk, or the "party." The state is regarded merely as an instrument for obtaining certain power positions. Thus it is deprived of any "objec-

15 May 23, 1935.

tivity" which might safeguard those who are to be oppressed.[16]
This anti-state attitude is taken up by American fascism and
becomes an "anti-government" attitude, nourished by the
hostility of American reactionaries to the New Deal. Here,
the old sectarian, anticentralistic spirit supplies a useful
weapon for the fight. Yet if the fascists have their way, the
actual result would be an enormous strengthening of the
state authority – a fact that should be pointed out to all
American particularists.

Such a general attitude is reflected by the Nazi hostility to the
big established churches. In Thomas' speeches, this antagonism often takes the form of an attack against the large institutionalized denominations, such as the Presbyterians, Methodists,
and Episcopalians, against whom he upholds his "subjectivistic,"
revivalist, "dynamic" concepts. He professes to stand for the
living faith against institutionalized religion, just as the Nazis
praise the "movement" against the State.[17] This stimulus
appeals to a deeply rooted discontent with all the supposedly
"objective," impersonal institutions of our society. Their objectivity appears to the masses as being rather problematic
anyway. The struggle against institutions is exemplified by the
present fight against "bureaucratism." The aim is not so much
to achieve a social justice which appears to be jeopardized
by institutionalism, as to call forth those violent instincts which
were held at bay by legal and institutional order, and which
are now let loose in order to become instruments of the power-
hunger of the dictatorial clique. It has often been pointed out
that monastic orders and sects were originally heretic movements, which only afterwards became integrated into the
Christian framework. One is perhaps justified in assuming
that an undercurrent of paganism, of a non-Christianized,

16 Cf. Franz Neumann, *Behemoth: The Structure and Practice of National
Socialism* (New York: Oxford University Press, 1942), passim, e. g.: "In
the new (Nazi) theory, the state has no monopoly of political decisions.
Schmitt concludes that the state no longer determines the political element
but is determined by it, that is, by the party" (p. 66). Neumann goes as far
as to deny that the German political system is at all a "state" (pp. 467–
470).

17 Cf. "Movement" trick [above, pp. 41-42].

non-civilized "religion of nature" is an intrinsic element of all sectarianism, no matter how ascetic and passionately Christian it may appear on the surface. At any rate, revivalist tradition is taken over and transformed by Thomas, in such a way that the destructive and naturalistic elements of anti-institutionalism are brought to the fore. While overplaying the Christian, he actually appeals to non-Christian instincts by his opposition to established, institutionalized religion. Thus, his racketeering in religion may be justly interpreted as a step towards the liquidation of religion, an unavoidable course for any totalitarian regime. This is why his manipulation of religious themes is more than a mere obsolete device to catch backward people. Behind his home-spun theology looms the spectre of a streamlined doctrine in which politics and ideologies are bluntly integrated in the name of "God, home, and the native land."

The basis for the fascist manipulation of religious subjectivism for political, ultimately antireligious purposes is the stressing of personal experience as against any objectified doctrine. Perhaps subsidiary to this is his emphasis on the apocalyptic mood. Some quotations from Thomas may illustrate his use of these elements:

Note that Jesus Christ places his words ... not in the old Testament words, not in the words of some writer, but his words ..... Now, I know, my friend, that this is true. I know it as the result of a number of reasons. I know it because of a personal experience that I had some twenty odd years ago with this living personality that we speak of as Jesus Christ. Now, I know it. I say to you from a personal experience. I believe that thing that Jesus has said here, that is I believe his word, if I expect his word, that I have here and now as a present-tense possession, eternal life. I know that because my life was immediately changed. The things that I loved from the standpoint of the flesh, I immediately hated. In other words, there was a complete transformation of my whole life and heart.[18]

It is significant that the emphasis upon Christ's personality and the subsequent "conversion" of the individual is brought into distinct antagonism with the Scriptures. By implication, the Old Testament is condemned as a sort of institutionalized,

18 June 7, 1935.

torpid religion. This attitude has recurred throughout Christian tradition since the Gnostics. Moreover, the appeal to immediate, personal religious experience means a weakening of rational control, as represented by coherent religious doctrines. Thomas insists upon the directness and immediacy of his personal relationship to God in order to exclude any interference from outside agencies: "God makes it very plain that no man should teach you because you have the Holy Spirit to teach you. I have insisted in my life upon being led directly by God himself."[19] It is easy to see how sectarian religiosity can be turned into an attack upon the Church and thus, ultimately, upon any organized, objective religion. The wish to be "led directly by God himself" can easily be misused as a justification for the most arbitrary decisions of the individual – just as Hitler referred to his "inspiration" when he committed his fateful error in the Russian campaign. Thomas' appeal to personal religious experience is bound up with anti-Semitic innuendo:

As I told you yesterday morning, membership in the Synagogue was synonymous with certain social rights of the day. Unless you belonged to the Synagogue, you were nobody. You were excluded from society as a whole. You did not have any ecclesiastical rights, no religious rights, no civil rights, and very few moral rights. Don't you see that they would exclude, and they had a monopoly upon the life and heart of the people of that day. The most devilish thing that this world knows anything about is where men have deliberately monopolized the power of God and the Gospel of God.[20]

The concept of personal conversion, as contrasted to institutionalized religion, is strengthened by the individual's belief in the imminence of a world catastrophe, of the "last days of the Church." This is the theological, revivalist basis of the "last hour" device. Faced with the last judgment, the individual must think of God and of his own immediate relationship to God, rather than of the Church to which he belongs. As already mentioned, Thomas in this respect does not shrink from appealing to the crudest superstition – a

19 June 18, 1935.
20 July 2, 1935.

striking symptom of the retrogression of his kind of revivalism into a sort of mythological nature religion.

The lines of prophesy are met.... I don't want you to become alarmed over the earthquakes we have had lately in Southern California (gives explanation of earthquakes of California as due to falls). Now, it used to be that we thought earthquakes were confined to Southern California, but we are finding across the world earthquakes, today, with a tremendous intensity and extensiveness.... Since 1901, over a million people have been killed as a result of earthquakes alone.[21]

Here, the interconnection between Thomas' terror technique and his religious "revivalism" can be grasped easily. The two major elements of this revivalism, subjectivism and Chiliasm, tend to "weaken" the individual's resistance. The appeal to "personal experience," as opposed to the doctrines of the Church, practically amounts to the encouragement of giving oneself up to one's emotions.[22] The idea that the world is nearing its end frightens the individual, who, in order to save his soul, is expected to be ready to do everything that he is told, without much critical thinking. Thus, the revivalist attitudes, originally conceived as an expression of religious liberty, are plainly put into the service of the fascist ideal of blind obedience.

"Anti-institution" trick

The transformation of religious subjectivism into fascist partisanship in Thomas' propaganda does not take place in terms of politics, for he is much too cautious to touch upon anything so firmly established as the American Constitutional Rights. Instead, he concentrates on his own narrow, quasi-professional field, church affairs. One may say that his attitude towards church problems, although never quite outspoken and somewhat confused, serves as an indirect model for what he secretly wants to take place within the American nation.

21 June 13, 1935.
22 Cf. "Emotional release" device [above, pp. 16-20].

He conveys totalitarian articles of faith to his audience by discussing church matters with them. He leaves it up to them to translate these statements into more drastic political terms. ˙ His revivalistic antagonism towards the established denominations is the theological vehicle that allows him to build up this "model" on apparently purely religious grounds.

Here, the "unity" trick triumphs. Thomas attacks "partisanship" and "disunity" under the name of denominationalism:

I believe that the day of denominations is practically a thing of the past. I mean there will be no further advancement along the lines of the denominations. I refer to Baptists, Congregationalists, Presbyterians, but listen, there is a great advancement today of a vital Christianity, and it is coming primarily as a result of the radio.[23]

The contrast between "vitality" and "denominationalism" is no less characteristic than the statement that this revitalization is due to radio, which is a centralistic technical device inseparably bound up with modern monopolization of public communications. The talk about "revitalization" corresponds to the idea that the existing religious denominations by their very institutionalization have ceased to be living forces, in other words, that the masses have lost their faith in those basic irrational doctrines of religion without which Protestantism cannot be conceived.

You know, my friend, organized religion that denies a supernatural will, will always persecute the supernatural, and so you had yonder a dead religion that denied the supernatural of God; and because they had that, they persecuted your Lord and my Lord unto death.[24]

It is not too difficult for Thomas' listeners to interpret this religious statement in terms of the two-party system and the "supreme" idea of the nation as such.

The logical sequel to such confused outbreaks would be the advocacy of strong enforcement of law against these anarchic spectres that he incessantly raises. It is a characteristically fascist twist in his propaganda, that just the opposite occurs. While deploring lawlessness, corruption, and anarchy, not only is he "antilegalistic" but he even attacks law as such. This

23 April 25, 1935.
24 June 29, 1935.

procedure, of course, is parallel to the well-known fascist device of crying wolf whenever a central democratic government shows any signs of strength. Their talk about the dictatorship of the government is simply a pretext for introducing their own dictatorship. Thomas' attitude towards law is highly ambivalent; he complains of the existing lawlessness as well as of the existing laws, in order to prepare psychologically the ground for some sort of non-"legalistic" rule.

Things are going wrong in this country of ours because we have forgotten God and his righteous law. We have trampled his standards of conduct and rule of judgment underfoot, and in its place we have enacted a host of human regulations. There is no dearth of law, today, my friends; this is the greatest age of legislative enactments to regulate man's conduct ever known in the history of this country. It is estimated that human government has made thirty-two million laws. There were ten thousand new laws placed on the statute books of the federal and state governments of the United States during 1924; there were thirteen thousand placed upon our statute books in 1928; fourteen thousand placed in 1930, and the last two years have multiplied these figures as a result of the New Deal which is the reign of law. But the greatest age of laws is also the greatest age of lawlessness. The criminal record shows that crime is increasing at a staggering rate. The direct cost of crime in this nation has reached fifteen billion dollars every year.[25]

The figures mentioned in this diatribe are, of course, utterly fantastic. There is neither any basis for the estimate of thirty-two million laws made by "human government" (whatever that may be), nor the slightest corroboration of the astronomical figure of the "cost of crime" in America. To operate with fantastic figures is an established Nazi habit. The apparent scientific exactitude of any set of figures silences resistance against the lies hidden behind the figures. This technique which might be called the "exactitude of error" device is common to all fascists. Phelps, for instance, has similar fantastic figures about the influx of refugees into this country. The greatness of the figure, incidentally, acts as a psychological stimulant, suggesting a general feeling of grandeur which is easily transfered to the speaker.

25 April 21, 1935.

His stress upon instinct against reason is concomitant to his emphasis on spontaneous behavior against laws and rules. Thus he promotes a spirit of "action" against the protection granted the minority by any kind of legal order. Indirectly, the antilegalistic and anti-institutional spirit of Thomas is strongly indicated by the way in which he exalts women. To choose one example among many: when praising Martha, he points out the unconventional spirit of this practical-minded saint, denouncing the sphere of convention by implication. Thomas exalts thereby an attitude which within the framework of his speeches is destructive, although in its highest sense it may be truly superior to conventionality. To Thomas unconventionality means, in the last analysis, readiness to break the law.

Martha, therefore, when she heard that Jesus was coming, went and met him. It was unconventional for a woman to go and meet a man but Martha, bless her soul and her heart, was unconventional. She refused to abide by a foolish convention that strangled the manifestation of her love, of her devotion.[26]

Officially, Thomas defends the home and the family and violently persecutes those who supposedly wish to "legalize abortion." Yet such statements come very close to the code of sex morals introduced by the Nazis who, while officially defending the sacred old institutions, encourage promiscuity as long as it helps to breed more *Volksgenossen*. Thomas' attack on law and convention does not aim at freedom, it aims at the individual's subjection, not to any independent legal or moral standards, but to the immediate dictation of those in command, who can easily dispense with any objective regulative ideas. He extols Martha's love in order to cloak the idea of obedience to commands. Such obedience would actually entail nothing but hatred.

26 July 9, 1935.

"Anti-Pharisees" device

Revivalist religious subjectivism glorifies the "spirit." Yet this
exaltation of the spirit should not be taken too seriously. It
is considerably softened by a twist closely related to Thomas'
intermittant attacks on the established churches: his denunciation of the Pharisees as the personification of religious institutionalism and faith in the "letter." The denunciation of the
Pharisees transfers hatred of law and institution to hatred of
the intellect and the intellectuals, and of the Jews, with
whom he indirectly identifies the Pharisees. He very cautiously
avoids explaining concretely what he means by spirit, but he
certainly implies a general enthusiasm and willingness to do
things rather than any specific capacity of the mind. The
Biblical preference for those who are weak in spirit, expressed
in Jesus' fight against the proud Pharisees, is exploited for
his own ends. There are unending invectives of this type:

My friend, this age has rejected the teaching of Jesus. Now, the
Church, the organized Church, has rejected the teaching of Jesus.
The Church that has adopted the teaching yonder of the hierarchy
of Israel, they have gone back to the intellect. Now, you know, all
you ought to know, that men by searching cannot find out God.
Your little puny intellect will not be able to find out the ministry of
God.[27]

Or:

I call your attention to the fact that Jesus never revealed his personality and his truth to men and women whose spirit was not right, and
will you think that out with me for a moment? To whom did he
reveal the mighty truths? ... Jesus revealed himself to that woman
because the woman was simple enough to believe the stories that
Jesus was telling the world.[28]

The Christian idea is that truth must be all-embracing, must
reach even the downtrodden. Thomas perverts it into the idea
of appealing to those "simple enough to believe the stories,"
because they are the least capable of offering any resistance to
untruth. This perversion, of course, has taken place throughout
the history of Christianity, but only today when fascism

27 June 20, 1935.
28 July 3, 1935.

adapts Christianity to its pragmatic purposes, has it been expressed so frankly and cynically.

In this respect, Thomas has a keen understanding of his affinity for his namesake, Martin Luther, whom he praises for having been, like St. Augustine, "just an obscure man" who would never have been chosen by "a group of intellectual leaders."[29] In fact, the defamation of the intellect is derived from the Augustinian and Lutheran tradition and is averse to Calvinism. It is hardly accidental that Thomas tends to side with Luther rather than with Calvin.

The Pharisees are particularly suitable objects for Thomas' intellect-baiting because they combine intellectual erudition and status as representatives of established religion. Moreover, their hostility to Christ makes it easy for Thomas to designate them as the vanguard of the Antichrist. The stimulus involved here is a resentment against the intellect. Those who must suffer, and have neither the strength nor the will to change their situation on their own impetus, always have a tendency to hate those who point out the negative aspects of the situation, that is, the intellectuals, rather than those who are responsible for their sufferings. This hostility is made the more intense by the fact that intellectuals are exempt from hard labor, without being in possession of actual commanding power. Therefore, they excite envy, without simultaneously calling forth deference. With Thomas' particular audience, anti-intellectualism has a particularly good chance of success. The Sermon on the Mount is transformed into an ideology for those who, while resenting their own hampered mentality, spitefully cling to and exalt this mentality.

This spitefulness is turned against the outsider, thus preparing the way for anti-Semitism. For the Jews are theologically close to Christianity without having submitted to it.

Now, you people, you see that Jesus Christ was a good man, that he was a chief rabbi of his day, that he was a great leader, but you refuse to acknowledge that he was God in human flesh. Remember that he cannot lie. Remember that the integrity of the Scriptures either stand or fall upon the evidence that is presented ("that all

29 May 31, 1935.

may honor the Son as they honor the Father"). My friend, you cannot approach God except through Jesus Christ, the Son of God. I know that is pretty hard on some of you people that have been taught otherwise. There is no way by which any man or woman may be saved except through Jesus Christ, and unless you honor the Son, you cannot honor the Father.[30]

Since the main difference between Christianity and Judaism concerns the recognition of the Son, this speech is, by implication, directed against the Jews. Incidentally, the "messenger" device is furthered by this particular theological doctrine. Of course, the stressing of this difference would not in itself be anti-Semitic. It becomes so in view of the fact that Thomas makes very few positive references to the relationship between the Old and the New Testaments. The idea that Christ did not come to dissolve, but to fulfill the law, that is, the Old Testament, is played down by Thomas. To him – and here he is certainly no fundamentalist – the New Testament is rather the denial of the Old:

There cannot be any immortality of the human soul according to the standard of the New Testament, according to the word of the living God, apart from the revelation and the work that Jesus Christ of Nazareth accomplished upon Calvary cross and from the tomb of Joseph of Arimathia.[31]

Instead of acknowledging the Old Testament, Thomas denounces it indirectly by putting a particular onus upon those who are "close" to Christianity without actually subscribing to it. Thus, by inference, he denounces the Jews.

Satan always attempts to reach the children of God by some member to that child of God. Satan knows that it is useless to make a direct attack upon the work of the living God, but he always attempts to reach that individual by someone that is close to that man or woman. Now, that was true of Judeah. You remember in the fourth chapter of Matthew, where it says that "Jesus vanquished the devil." If you turn over to the book of Luke, you will find yonder in the hour when the Last Supper was being held, Satan came and entered into Judas Iscariot. He said, I cannot reach him directly, but I must ask the death of Jesus Christ through someone that is close to him.[32]

30 June 6, 1935.
31 June 7, 1935.
32 July 13, 1935.

This whole passage, particularly the associational link between the words Judeah, Judas, Jews, points in the direction of the whole "anti-Pharisees" device by its identification of the Jews with the Christ-killer.

Religious trickery in operation

It is our basic thesis that religion, while being used as a net to ensnare a certain group of the population, is also transformed into a technique of political manipulation. Thomas contends in one passage that "Satan has not the power, today, over the Christian, for he has met his Waterloo at Calvary."[33] This figure of speech, subordinating religious salvation to an earthy event, is symbolic of Thomas' treatment of religion. One may say that he transforms Calvary into an eternal Waterloo, so that his religion deteriorates into a system of metaphors for mundane "battles," for political violence. His sophistic art of interpreting the Bible for the sake of ideas which are essentially incompatible with the spirit of Christianity often amounts to caricature. The complete cynicism with which he handles Biblical stories shows that he is actually concerned only with the residues of religious prestige and authority. He has no interest whatsoever in the concrete substance of religion. It goes without saying that the subordination of religious ideas and religious language to political ends deeply affects the religious ideas themselves. Calvary, by being called a Waterloo, loses that quality of uniqueness which constitutes the faith in the crucifixion as the act of redemption. The very metaphor, apart from any further dogmatic consequences, must have a ring of impiety to any Christian. It is essential to point out those Christians whom fascist propaganda intends to reach, that fascist manipulation of the dogma is intrinsically blasphemous.

The blasphemous element becomes even more blatant with regard to the contents of the Biblical stories Thomas uses. For

33 May 24, 1935.

example, the supernatural meaning of the Biblical concept of "feeding the people" is perverted into an expression of a merciless and hard-boiled attitude in earthly matters.

Our Lord, Jesus Christ, is not a bread-king. He is not feeding people for the sake of feeding them. "Whatsoever you do in word and in deed, do all to the glory of God." You know, my friend, that you and I make a tremendous mistake, and we do that person more harm than good when we confer upon that individual something he does not need. It does not matter what it is, whether it is the dole, whether it is free money, and we do for that individual that which that individual can do for himself. You rob that individual of the blessing of life. You rob that individual of the joy of working. We have got to end our present situation . . . in some way, manner, or form. If we do not, we will continue to pauperize millions of people in this country of ours.[34]

Likewise, the idea that Jesus is the bread of life is perverted into a denunciation of other sources of the spirit, namely, autonomous thought in general and ideas of reform in particular. Characteristically, however, Thomas, while attacking enlightenment, does not dare to attack technology at the same time, for the latter is a presupposition and a living element of his own propaganda technique.

My, I wish we could recall America to know this today [sic]. Many people are running to this thing and to that thing, running to this quack and to that quack, and they are getting nowhere. Here is the true bread of life. I am sure that your soul knows that. How many people throughout the world are trying to find truth, the true aims in life besides Jesus Christ. Attend to God. Apart from him, you cannot get great truth. I would to God, that we would get this great truth. Don't you wish that education would get back. I thank God, that we have a mighty God. Thank God for the printing press. Thank God for the newspaper. Thank God today, and take courage, for our God is still on his throne, and I believe that we are firing a shot that will be heard around the world.[35]

The confusion of these sentences faithfully reflects the entanglement of ideas of a bigot running berserk. He advocates both the "good old times" and the radio which gives him the opportunity to speak.

Faith, to Thomas, is not only a substitute for changing the

34 June 12, 1935.
35 June 13, 1935.

world; it is the medicine to counteract any change at all. Moreover, all change is automatically pigeonholed by Thomas as Communism.

> Can you not see that unless we exalt the holiness of our God, that unless we proclaim the justice of God in this world of ours, unless we proclaim the fact of a heaven and of a hell, unless we proclaim the fact that without the remission, *without the shedding of blood,* there is no remission of sin. Cannot you see that only Christ and God are dominant and that revolution will ultimately take this nation of ours.[36]

The transformation of Christian doctrines into slogans of political violence could not be cruder than in this passage. The idea of the Sacrament, the "shedding of blood" of Christ, is straightforwardly interpreted in terms of "shedding of blood" in general, with an eye to a political upheaval. The actual shedding of blood is advocated as necessary because the world has supposedly been redeemed by the shedding of Christ's blood. Murder is invested with the halo of a Sacrament. Thus the last remainder of the sacrificed Christ is virtually *"Judenblut muß fließen."* The crucifixion is degraded into a symbol of the pogrom. There are strong reasons for believing that this absurd transformation plays a greater role in traditional Christian imagery than appears on the surface.

"Faith of our fathers" device

The most effective link between Thomas' theology and his politics is the idea of the "faith of our fathers." This idea may be called essentially anti-Christian. The claim of Christianity is a claim to truth and not to traditional acceptance, so that he who believes only because his forefathers have believed is actually not a believer at all. Incidentally, the idea of the forefathers carries overtones of an ancestor worship and a mythological religion of nature which contradict the very essence of Christianity. Yet this "naturalistic" element of Christianity can be found throughout Protestantism (where

36 July 13, 1935.

it substitutes for the Catholic concept of the living Church). Even the most subjectivistic Lutheran thinkers, such as Kierkegaard, have made use of this idea. Paternalistic authority always functions to keep at bay those whose belief in the truth of the Christian dogma itself is shattered. This device enforces Christianity by worldly, extraneous means, in the last analysis, by the controls of the patriarchal family. At the same time, it sounds highly respectable, humble, and pious. This appeal is the backbone of Thomas' orthodoxy, opening the road for an interpretation which can easily be understood in terms of aggressive nativism.

That Book that has united the souls of millions of men and women everywhere, that old Book that our fathers and our mothers loved, that old Book that they have revered and cared for, and that we, today, this generation now living, we too are perusing the old Book, so as we look into its sacred pages, this afternoon, bring unto us the memories of the past and the hope of the future and prepare us for that heaven whither our fathers and our mothers have traveled all of these long years.[37]

The next stage is the ambiguous definition of America as a "Christian nation" by which Thomas refers to a supposed decision of the Supreme Court which pronounced such a definition. Thomas strongly implies the exclusion of the Jews from the American community.

Listen, America began as a Christian nation. Whatever has developed in this nation of ours in the way of progress is the result of Americanism, and when you speak of America, you have got to speak of Christianity because they are both commensurate.[38]

And here Thomas utters the call for the "right sort of people"–evidently the same characters who paved the way for Nazism in Germany:

I call upon you teachers, this afternoon, to remember that you hold in your hand the future of America. "As the Twig is bent, so cometh a tree, and as the tree falleth, so it will lie." We need teachers to teach the great principle of life. We need to declare the great truth of God. We need judges upon our benches who will remember the landmarks of their fathers are still here.[39]

37 June 23, 1935.
38 May 26, 1935.
39 June 2, 1935.

It is hardly necessary to point out that these teachers and judges are expected to be severe. The traditionalistic stimulus in Thomas is so strong that in spite of his supposed hatred for denominations and conventions, he maintains that "the only way to worship God is to go a place dedicated to worship."[40] Such a statement, which is in accordance with Roman Catholic teaching rather than with the Protestant doctrine of "universal priesthood" (*Allgemeines Priestertum*), is another index of Thomas' use of Christianity as a mere analogy for his worldly authoritarianism.

It is but one step from worship of the "fathers" and a "Christian" America to arrogant patriotism: "We are dependent upon our God and those who believe in this country and in this Bible and in your family and in your flag and in these freedom-loving institutions that have been handed down to us."[41] Thomas' ultimate desire for a military pattern, for an authoritarian organization is hardly disguised in a "hymn" which his boys sing.

> Where are the boys of the old brigade,
> Who fought with us side by side
> Shoulder by shoulder
> And blade to blade.
> They fought till they fell and died
> Who so ready and undismayed
> Who so merry and true.
> Where are the boys of the old brigade
> And where is the land we knew?
> It was steadily shoulder to shoulder,
> And steadily blade to blade
> Ready in song
> Marching along
> Were the boys of the old brigade.
>
> Praise be their memory wherever they are;
> They were the comrades we shall ever love.[42]

40 July 6, 1935.
41 June 16, 1935.
42 July 7, 1935.

While, on the surface, military symbolism is used in order to illustrate religious ideals, religion itself for Thomas functions as the symbol of fascism. The Christian American Crusade promises both revivalism and orthodox Christianity. Their common denominator in propaganda is fascist organization.

SECTION IV:
Ideological Bait

Introductory Remarks

As it has been pointed out, the concrete political content of Thomas' speeches plays but a minor role compared with his method. His psychological "softening up" of his listeners in the fascist sense does not develop any coherent political program or any coherent critique of existing social and political conditions. His whole attitude is thoroughly "atheoretical." This is due partly to his contempt for the intellectual capacity of his audience, partly to the idea of "being practical," and partly, perhaps, to the actual absence of a clear-cut program in Thomas' mind. Like most of today's fascist agitators, he is essentially guided by a keen sense of imitation of the famous and successful models of modern authoritarianism, rather than by political or sociological reflections. This atheoretical attitude has been noted since the early days of the Mussolini regime. It may have a deep basis in the pattern of authoritarianism itself. It cannot be simply explained by the cynical, relativistic contempt for truth and for its expression in theory, shown by the uninhibited power-politician. It is rather due to theory in itself, no matter what its contents may be. The very fact of consequent, coherent and consistent thinking carries a certain weight of its own, a certain "objectivity," even if it starts from the most arbitrary presumptions. This objectivity makes theory a problematic tool in the eyes of the fascist, for the reason that thinking *per se* refuses to become completely a tool. Theory as such, the pursuit of autonomous logical processes, offers a certain guarantee to those at whom the fascist wants to strike – it allows them, as it were, to be heard. Hence, theory is essentially taboo to the fascist. His realm is that of unrelated, opaque, isolated facts, or rather, images of facts. The more they are presented as isolated, the more some selected favorite topics draw the whole attention of both the agitator and the listeners, the better for the fascist. He may, with good chance of success, simultaneously but atheoretically, hit at both the Jewish banker and the Jewish radical. If he would try theoretically to explain the interconnection between the notions, he would meet the greatest difficulties. He would be forced to take resort to the most unconvincing constructs — something which happens often enough with fascist propaganda. Thomas, however, tries to dodge this danger as far as possible, and to stick to some few well-tested and thoroughly popular tunes. This may partly explain the scarcity of motives not only in Thomas but in most of his type. It requires special countermeasures, such as "relating" the isolated topics in order to explode them, concentrating the arguments on the danger spots, or perhaps, conversely, bringing to the fore those facts and structures which are omitted in the fascist argument. Whatever Thomas does is in order to hit at certain "nerve points" of political controversy, which are particularly touchy and from the manipulation of which he hopes to get quick emotional returns. The political topics he chooses are those which he expects to be most important psychologically, that is to say, those which are most heavily laden with effects. These are Communism, the Administration and in particular its unemployment policy, the Jews, and certain aspects of foreign policy.

Imagery of Communism

It has been stated over and over again that the attack on the danger of Communism and radicalism is one of the fundamentals of fascist propaganda. This line of attack has proved most effective in Hitler's case. Naturally all the paraphernalia of "red-baiting" are to be found in Thomas' speeches. For example, he employs the device of denouncing anyone as a Communist who disagrees with his own ideas. This is mainly achieved by the use of the term "radical," which in fact can mean anyone who follows a progressive line, but which has a connotation of revolutionary subversiveness, highly useful for Thomas' propaganda.

The anti-Communist arguments common to fascists all point in one direction, namely, that Communism is an immediate danger, that the traditional institutions of property, family, and religion must be defended by immediate counteraction. One thing, however, is remarkable. Thomas never deals with Communism as it actually is. He attacks neither the doctrines of dialectical materialism, of which he apparently knows nothing, nor the practical policy of the Communist party, nor the real conditions in Russia. He never touches upon fundamental questions, such as whether a classless society is possible under contemporary conditions, or whether the lot of the masses has improved in Russia. The ideals crystalized by Marxian theory are never scrutinized. Instead, he builds up the imagery of Communism as a "bogy," which exists only to terrify people with the vision of their immediate destruction. He does not attack the Marxian system, except in vaguest generalizations concerning such matters as materialism. But he tells atrocity stories of an utterly fantastic nature, similar to the "Protocols of the Elders of Zion." He fights against windmills or, if one prefers the term, he builds up a paranoic system which he later attacks. This mechanism is of particular importance, since it shows the deep-rooted tendency in fascism to attack images rather than the reality they may represent. The foes of fascism are largely of a fictitious nature for two reasons. On the one hand, the reality of groups such as the Communists or the Jews would probably not provide sufficient objects of hatred. If Thomas were to discuss Communist theory as it really is, the effect might well be that his listeners would become positively interested in the theory. On the other hand, he consciously or unconsciously reckons with a "paranoic" attitude among his listeners, a kind of persecution mania which craves the confirmation of its bogies. Knowing that he can get hold of his followers only by satisfying this craving, he cuts his imagery to fit their psychological desires. The general scheme of this imagery is the characterization of

Communism as a conspiracy. This concept being a mirrored reflection of the conspiratorial character of his own racket.

We lay particular emphasis on this aspect since it is not only the pattern of red-baiting but also, to an even higher degree, of anti-Semitism. The unrecognizable and nauseating caricatures contained in the *"Stürmer"* are characteristic of the whole fascist approach. The psychological attack is directed not so much against the Jews as they actually are, as against a mythical picture of the Jews, an amalgam of observations, remnants of an archaic imagery, and projections of psychological drives. In olden times, a magic picture was destroyed in order to kill the man it represented. Today we may almost say that the converse is true – the Jews themselves are destroyed in order to harm the image. Therefore, it may often be not so appropriate to defend the Jews against objections which finally aim at a fetish, as to point out the fetishistic nature of the fascist concept of "The Jew." It is important to show the elements of this fetish and their relative independence of reality, to examine its psychological function, etc. Only thus may this image be dissolved effectively. It will remain largely impervious to any defense of the actual Jews[1] since anti-Semitism is based less upon Jewish peculiarities than upon the mentality of the anti-Semite.

The transformation of Communism into a sinister conspiracy is achieved by passages such as the following:

I wonder if you people know that Stalin, Joseph Stalin, last year, now get it, last year, he published a plan for the destruction of the United States of America. This information was passed on to all of the Communist destruction organizers and secretaries.[2] Now read it. And then review in your mind what has taken place and what is increasingly taking place all over this nation. You note the action of

1 A German joke, fairly popular in pro-Hitler days, expresses this idea quite appropriately: "The Jews are guilty."–"No, the bicyclists."–"Why the bicyclists?"–"Why the Jews?" The motive behind this joke, which is by no means very "witty" but strikes at an essential point, should be followed up carefully by counterpropaganda.

2 The mentioning of "all the organizers and secretaries" is apparently the projection of a bureaucratic wish-fantasy on Thomas' part. It is he who always wants to organize, and dreams of having innumerable secretaries.

certain Congressmen. You note the action of certain Senators. You
note the action of certain leaders in our country. Then, you decide
for yourself the seriousness of the hour. Here are the Devil's sugges-
tions: Now, I am going to give them to you as far as I can during
the next few minutes. (This passage is evidently an appetizer, indica-
ting that he expects his listeners to get quite a kick out of what he is
going to reveal to them.) He (Stalin) says in the realm of religion:
"By philosophy and mysticism, by the development of liberal cults
and by the furtherance of atheism, we must destroy all Christian
creeds."[3]

The pure nonsense of this quotation fits well with the fantastic
allegations by which it is preceded.

As far as Marxian theory is concerned, Thomas copes with it
in a simple way:

Listen, my friend, what may we expect when we teach our children
that man has no soul, when we teach them such doctrines as Karl
Marx's Manifesto. This has prepared the world for the final teaching of Communism, my friends, we are going into hell in this country
of ours. We have allowed this teaching, this terrible teaching to
saturate this country of ours. It has saturated the whole home (!), it
has saturated the school. We have allowed our curriculum to be
based upon this hypothesis that man has no soul and that by organic
evolution, by some way or another man came and all life came upon
the earth. ... We must turn quickly from this teaching or we are
lost ... that is teaching the foundation stones of Communism.[4]

It is significant that in describing Communist teachings neither
the concept of class struggle nor of capitalistic economy is even
mentioned. The emphasis is laid upon biological theories which
never played any decisive role in Marxian theory, or upon
wholly imaginative attributions to Marx.

"Communists and bankers" device

Thomas' most important horror story refers to supposed
plots intended to produce financial crises and bankruptcy.
When he discusses the Communist attitude towards property,
he does not bring in the concept of socialization, but only that

3 June 16, 1935.
4 June 10, 1935.

of a manipulation by which people lose all their possessions. The typical fascist identification of the "Communist conspiracy" with the "bankers' conspiracy" is useful primarily for the sake of anti-Semitism.

A few years ago men met. Let me give you the plan and the program. Listen to what they say: "We have opened the arenas in different states where revolts are now occuring, and disorder and bankruptcy will shortly appear everywhere." That was just prior to 1929, that we saw this thing approaching the U.S. My friend, nation after nation is collapsing. We saw the collapse of nation after nation. We saw the capitals of the world, my friend, in a turmoil. Now, we have seen it occur in these United States of ours. "Disorders and bankruptcy will appear shortly everywhere." Listen to what they say. "We will present ourselves in the guise of saviors of the workers from oppression when we suggest that they enter our army of socialists, anarchists and Communists to whom we always extend our hand under the guise of the rule of brotherhood." (Although Thomas dresses up such statements as quotations, he never gives any exact references. It is most likely that he quotes from fascist papers or pamphlets, for nothing is more ridiculous than the picture of a supposedly official Communist linking "socialists, anarchists, and Communists.") Is not that the thing that they had done for our nation? Is not that what caused the collapse of bank after bank and bank after bank until, my friend, it has been estimated that thousands of banks have failed in these United Sates.[5]

Marxian theory explains the crisis as being caused by the instrinsic laws of capitalistic production. Fascism hits back by attributing the crisis to Communist manipulation. But fascism does not take the trouble to point out how these devilish schemes could work, or how the Communists could possibly control the economic life of America, as long as the capitalistic system prevails. The only possible explanation left to his audience, though not expressly stated, is that a certain group of capitalists, to wit the financiers, are conspiring with the Communists. This device has several advantages. First of all, it serves to discredit Communism which appears no longer as a comprehensive social system, but rather as the opposite, a shrewd trick for profiteering rackets. Conversely, it accuses one particular selected capitalist group, that of "non-produc-

5 June 30, 1935.

tive capital," of undermining the principle of private property
which the bankers, as businessmen are supposed to represent.
The obvious objection, that no capitalist group would plot
against the system from which its own profit is derived, should
strike everyone exposed to such propaganda. The absurdity
of this device does not prevent its recurrence throughout
fascist propaganda – in one of his esoteric speeches, for instance,
Thomas warms up the old story that some international Jewish
bankers financed the Bolshevik revolution. Obviously, this
formula must have some very powerful irrational, psychological backing. It is certainly the easiest way to combine hatred
of the Jews as capitalists with their denunciation as subversive
radicals. Many people distrust bankers because transactions
on the stock exchange, particularly sudden booms and slumps,
used to be largely incomprehensible to them. Since they often
had to suffer under such moves, they tended to personify the
anonymous reasons for financial losses and to blame acquisitive,
plotting groups.
Formerly the operations of the stock exchange actually had a
largely "irrational," unplanned character, which they partly
lost in the era of economic concentration. Yet, the attitude
against the financier has become habitual and assumes a
threatening aspect, in an epoch when "finance capital" appears
to lose much of the power which it may have held during the
nineteenth century. One may even go so far as to presume
that modern hatred against the banker is actually caused by
the feeling that he is no longer the power he used to be, and
that he can be easily done away with. Imagery of the banker's
omnipotence rationalizes the dawning feeling of his impotence.
As for the Communists, the idea that they are conspirators
and criminals is grounded in their hostility to the whole
capitalist system. This attitude forces upon the Communists
certain restrictions in formulating their aims and tactics, and
thus makes them appear "mysterious" in the eyes of many.
Since the fight against "non-productive" capital is one of the
most effective stimuli of anti-Semitism, it will be necessary to
cope with this question explicitly in other parts of our project.
Here we confine ourselves to two observations. First, the

finance capitalist draws hatred upon himself because he appears to enjoy life und luxury without holding, as the industrialist does, any actual commanding power. Second, the "intermediary," the middleman – of whom the "omnipotent banker" is but an enlarged symbol – is the person who makes the underlying population pay for economic processes which actually take place within the sphere of production. The intermediary has the function of a psychological and economic scapegoat, a function zealously kept alive by certain economic interests. It goes without saying that these hypotheses can be proved only by a full-fledged economic critique of the entire distinction between productive and non-productive capital. At this point, they may only illustrate why the rationally "absurd" identification of banker and Communist proves to be so effective.

As we pointed out, Thomas does not enter into any economic controversy. There is one point, however, where he becomes specific. It is at just this point that he distorts the actual content of Marxian teachings into its opposite. As is well known, Marxism calls for the socialization of the means of production, without proposing the idea that small personal property should be expropriated. Since Thomas' listeners do not own any considerable "means of production" and are only small owners, the idea of the socialization of industry would not be so frightening to them. Therefore, socialism must be depicted as an attempt to deprive them of the little they have, rather than as an attempt to substantially improve the standard of living of the whole population. The Communist is identified with the robber and the thief – in fact, with those looters who usually follow the wake of fascist upheavals.

The second thing the Communists expect to do (the first being, according to Thomas, the universal introduction of atheism) is to destroy all private property and inheritance. They have taken us subtly and wilyly. They say, all private property and inheritance has to be done away with. That means the nationalization of every foot of property. That means the confiscation of everything that you and I hold dear.[6]

6 April 25, 1935.

This argument, incidentally, is probably one of the most effective in enrolling the little man into the ranks of fascism.

One last device of Thomas' red-baiting ought to be mentioned. It stems from the Nazi arsenal. One line of the Horst Wessel *Lied* reads: "*Kam'raden, die Rotfront und Reaktion erschossen.*" Thomas often embellishes his tirades against Communists by some hostile references to "reaction," although this reference never carries the same emphasis as red-baiting. The reason is, on the one hand, that the poor to whom this propaganda is addressed may become suspicious if only Communism is attacked. Hence the real point is clouded by impressing the conviction that old-fashioned reactionaries, groups who do not properly take care of the masses, are also regarded as foes. On the other hand, there is a certain, very slight, realistic basis for reactionary-baiting in fascism. This is the fascist antagonism to certain rival conservative groups with whom they often have to ally themselves, but whom they ultimately liquidate, as they did most effectively in Germany. The antireactionary window-dressing of red-baiting is expressed by Thomas in a concrete political situation:

Take the school board as an illustration. It seems to me as though the public is going to take a whipping either way it goes. There are two tickets, one known as the security ticket, consisting of Mr. Becker, Mr. Dalton, Mrs. Clark, and Mrs. Roundsville; they have the backing of a number of the old reactionary groups. Now, I seriously question, tonight, whether that group will have the power to really clear up the school situation in this city.[17]

On another occasion, Thomas puts it in more general terms: "I want you people to pray, today, very definitely, that the forces of reaction and the forces that seek to put Christ down may not be allowed to close the radio to the people of God."[8] Thomas wants to drive the Communists out of the United States; but in order to do this, and to prepare for violent action against them, he wants to take over at least their revolutionary concept and attitudes. He attacks reaction because he wants to act by non-legal means – by mob violence and

7 April 29, 1935.
8 May 24, 1935.

"spontaneous action." On the one hand, the masses whom the fascist agitator addresses are skeptical of the old ruling class, which they have been accustomed to regard as their master and exploiter. On the other hand, the old ruling class – no matter how the interest of the fascist movement may be related to its own – appears to be unfit for the brutal business of immediate oppression which is fascist government. Cultural tradition, social "status," even snobbery bar the upper class at least to a certain extent from those attitudes by which authoritarianism rules. Hence, the ruling class is sometimes defamed by fascists as arrogant and "alien to the folk." Apart from this superficial issue, there exist definite rivalries between the old and the new "elites" – between those who own big property and those who "protect" and, to a considerable extent, control it by their terror apparatus. Thus *"Reaktion,"* the old ruling class, serves very well the propagandistic purpose of drawing upon itself radical trends of the masses without any serious danger to the authoritarian setup. For it should be noted that, in contrast to the baiting of the "Jewish banker," fascist propaganda against "reaction" remains rather general and very rarely leads to actual conflict, except in extremely critical situations. Thomas is cautious enough to speak about the *"old* reactionary groups" only, leaving the door open for their acceptance into his own more up-to-date version.

Administration- and President-baiting

There is quite a treasure of subjects at hand for government-baiting by fascist groups. Government by representation can always be depicted as "indirect," alien to the people, cold and institutionalized.[9] Its centralistic nature always can be played up as being directed against the interest of the people, particularly those living in the more distant section. There is the bogy of "bureaucracy" which can be dug up wherever a

9 Cf. p. 98, above.

centralized democratic government has to cope with the nice-
ties of rational and constitutional law. Then there is always the
possibility of calling such a government wasteful or corrupt.
Every expenditure is likely to appear as "waste" to the little
man who must pay taxes without being able to see how this
money works for his immediate advantage. The mentality of
the actually or supposedly overburdened taxpayer, and his
inherent antagonism to centralized government are psychological assets of fascist propaganda. A feeling of injustice is
involved in tax-paying under an anonymous state which
takes without being capable of guaranteeing the lives of those
from whom it takes. Even people with only meager direct
taxes, as is probably true of Thomas' audience, may often
share the taxpayer mentality through their desire to ape economic superiors. The "overburdened taxpayer" tends to become a
creed of its own. The consequent resentment is directed
towards the government that takes rather than towards a
social system which makes taxes unavoidable. Of course,
where fascism comes into power, even heavier taxes will have
to be paid, but they are more effectively cloaked, at least at
the beginning, as being love offerings for the immediate benefit
of the fatherland and racial comrades. The reference to the
idea of the folk together with terror, temporarily stops any
discussion of the tax issue. The same applies to the issue of
corruption. There is no doubt that there is more waste
and corruption in countries where uncontrolled, domineering
groups are in power, than in democratic nations. In totalitarian
countries corruption cases are kept hidden, and the subject
rarely comes up. The fact that democracies allow frank
discussion of corruption creates the illusion that democracy is
the breeding ground of corruption. Naturally, the "progressive," pointedly democratic Roosevelt Administration is a
particularly adequate target for the antigovernmental attitude
of fascists, although one should by no means think that fascist
opposition is essentially bound up with the New Deal. Liberal
Republicans like Wendell Willkie are now attacked in a
similar way. However, fascist propaganda against the New
Deal can feed upon the liberal tradition of the United States

which regards any state interference in economic matters as a means of denouncing the present.

Thomas hates the President and wants his audience to hate him. Yet he always speaks about "our President" and prays for him, thus professing to honor the tolerant tradition of American democracy. However, there is actually only one thing he wants the President to do: to repent. The Christian idea of repentance is transformed into a shrewd means of blackening the Chief Executive:

My friend, I speak to you in the most solemn way that it is possible to address a human being, that unless you repent, unless the President of the United States repents, unless the Supreme Court repents, unless the members of the Senate repent, etc.,unless every man and woman of this nation repents, you cannot see the Kingdom of God.[10]

It may be assumed that in this passage "every man and woman" is incidental and that the real emphasis is laid upon the President who has never left any doubt of his basically liberal convictions.

By innuendo the President and his Administration – or at least some "high places" – are linked up with Communism. This device, by the way, is by no means limited to fascist agitators, but is used by practically all foes of the Administration: "Why will America stand for this type of thing (an artificially organized economic crisis)? Is it possible that in high places, my friend, that encouragement has been lent to this type of thing?"[11] The title of one of his speeches puts the stigma of Communism squarely upon the shoulder of the Administration: "Is it true, as charged by the U.S. Chamber of Commerce, that Communism is the real aim of many of those around our President?"[12] In one of his "esoteric" speeches, Thomas goes so far as to allege that, even though the "Protocols of the Elders of Zion" have been proved to be falsifications, their inner truth is proved by the New Deal. The Administration has supposedly executed step by step all the plans laid down in those documents. Incidentally, exactly the same argument

10 June 14, 1935.
11 June 30, 1935.
12 July 14, 1935.

was put forward by the Nazi, Rosenberg, when he maintained the inner truth of these protocols, after their falsity had been acknowledged by a Swiss Court. Rational refutation is psychologically powerless against such legends as that of the protocols, or such insinuations as those made against the Administration by Thomas. As soon as they cannot be maintained any longer on the objective level, they are transformed by auxiliary hypotheses, or by shifting from the level of facts to the level of "inner truth."

President-baiting is by no means new in the United States. It has recurred again and again since the days of Andrew Johnson, and historical analysis would probably reveal a permanent readiness to indict the President on the part of certain political groups. Ironically enough, the baiters of Johnson called themselves "radicals." The thesis that the attitude of the population towards the President is ambivalent because he is a father image appears to us unspecific and simplistic. Modern monarchies such as Great Britain show few analogies to President-baiting in republics. The habit stems rather from certain issues of democracy in general, and of the American Constitution in particular. The fact that government "of the people, by the people and for the people" invests one single individual with the considerable power of the presidency is apparently paradoxical in the eyes of many people. Unconsciously at least, a strong resistance is elicited. *Prima facie,* the chief executive power is resented as reminiscent of monarchism, as "undemocratic." Hence the constant readiness to invoke the system of checks and balances against the executive branch, to say that it oversteps its boundaries and craves dictatorship. Today, however, this old resistance of primitive or "folk" democracy to the idea of representation and the institution of the Presidency serves mainly to promote an utterly different ideology. What is actually resented about the President is not so much his "antidemocratic" power as the idea that this power is not "legitimate," that his authority is not the genuine expression of today's basic power relationships. Therefore, the fascist-minded want it to be destroyed. Old memories of absolutistic legitimacy have been converted into the fascist idea once expressed by Goebbels, that only one who makes use of power deserves it, that is to say, one who exploits it for the purpose of ruthless oppression. While the President is denounced as a would-be dictator, he is actually despised because he will not, and cannot, act dictatorially, since he represents a system, and groups, which are intrinsically antidictatorial. In the last analysis, the President-baiters sense somehow that the legal power invested in the President does not fully correspond to his actual social power – that the decisive economic forces are to be found beyond his range and, at the present time, in the other camp. Hence his constitutional rights are psychologically conceived as being "illegitimate," compared with big ownership, which expresses the essence of business culture. Modern President-baiting is an index of the conflict between formal democracy and economic concentration, a conflict which tends to increase proportionately with the latter. The history of the French Third Republic in particular, where the official democratic regime permanently was snubbed not only by the old aristocracy but also by the most influential economic forces, is highly analogous to modern American President-baiting. In a way, hatred of the President is not altogether different from that against high finance, with which the fascist like to link him.

"Pick up thy bed and walk" device

In addition to President-baiting and the general assumption that the Roosevelt Administration encourages atheism, Communism, and modernism, there is actually only one specific point attacked by Thomas – the unemployment policies of the New Deal. In this respect Thomas is definitely old-fashioned and appeals to groups of small property owners: He fails to recognize the gravity of the unemployment problem and the pressures in it which can be used, whereas more modern fascists, such as Phelps, try to win over the unemployed to the "movement." It is probably this aspect of Thomas' propaganda which is largely responsible for his failure, though, on

the other hand, this aspect also attracted groups which otherwise might have been hostile to his whole approach. Propagandistic exploitation of the problem of unemployment and
actual fascist "integration" of the unemployed are two very
different things. Thomas carefully cloaks his anti-unemployed
attitude in Christian terms. Interpreting the sentence "Arise,
pick up thy bed and walk" in terms of professional initiative
completely alien to the Bible, Thomas says:

God says to walk. We have killed the spirit of tens of thousands of
people by dispensing charity. We are never going to solve America's
problems except those people who are in actual need be given help.
On a certain day, at a certain hour, at a certain minute, at a certain
second, if we say every dollar is going to give you so much time
and by then, by the Grace of God, if you don't want work, you
don't want to eat. It is almost impossible to get a man or woman to
work. We have got to stop this situation.[13]

Exactly the same device has worked in Germany. Naturally
the unemployed had to be fed there too, but the difference in
Germany was that they had to "work" for it for a short period
by doing unnecessary and futile work, and later by preparing
the war of aggression. The idea that no one should be allowed
to eat without working, although the work in itself may be
utterly superfluous, has proved most attractive psychologically. One of the paradoxes of the present situation is that envy
is concentrated upon the most unfortunate group, the unemployed, because they are conceived of as being exempted
from the hardship of labor. This envy works as a tool to bring
the unemployed as "soldiers of labor" under the immediate
control of the domineering group, while offering a certain
gratification to the actual job-holders. Thomas' hatred
against the Administration stems largely from this source. The
idea of forcing the unemployed to work is occasionally
presented by Thomas in the form of some phoney appeal for
agrarian reform, showing his affinity to the "blood and soil"
ideology.

The government should supply the means of production and furnish
the individuals with ten acres of ground – or whatever they are able

13 June 3, 1935.

to do – and let them get out and by the sweat of their brows[14] earn their daily bread. There are millions of people in this country at the present hour who do not want to work. There are millions of people in this country who don't want to work and who would not accept a position if they had that opportunity.[15]

The unemployed are depicted as lazy. Thomas proclaims the need for a strong hand. By implication, a fascist regime appears to be the only chance of teaching them to work, of "integrating" them, and simultaneously of punishing them for their laziness. One should expect, *prima facie,* that the cynicism of such statements would alienate the masses and produce violent opposition to Thomas. Although this may have happened with some of his listeners, it would be too rationalistic to assume that it played a large role. Thomas is shrewd enough to reckon with a paradoxical longing for the strong hand among those who would have to feel its strength. They enjoy authority not only because it gives them a feeling of security, but also because they identify themselves so strongly with the power system that they are ready to undergo any hardship, as proof of the power and virility with which their own humiliation seems to incorporate them. In imperial Germany many ex-soldiers, who had suffered the most brutal treatment under Prussian militarism, later on referred to military service as the most beautiful time of their lives. Such is the attitude which Thomas calculates upon in his attack on the unemployed. There are no means of checking this phenomenon, but it would not be astonishing to discover that he enrolled a considerable number of followers from the ranks of those whom he whipped for their supposed unwillingness to work. Moreover, it is probably these same followers who are most prone to excesses against the weak.

14 Exactly the same expression is used by Luther in his book against the Jews, where he advocates subjecting them to forced labor. (Cf. Institute of Social Research, *Studies in Philosophy and Social Science,* ed. Max Horkheimer, IX, 1941, p. 128.)
15 June 12, 1935.

The Jews are coming

In Thomas' propaganda over the radio, anti-Semitism is
only a sideshow. He is hampered not only by the regulations of
broadcasting but also by the religious medium. In a certain
way, his religious line calls for respect by the people for the
Old Testament and is irreconcilable with too frank an attack
upon a minority group. Yet the esoteric speeches show that
Thomas is, or at least was, violently anti-Semitic. By innuendo,
his anti-Semitism is also expressed in his radio addresses.
Taking into consideration his vocal inflection and oratorical
attitude, it can be assumed that he refers to the Jews when he
speaks about "these forces" and suggests that his audience
knows what he means. The weight of the anti-Semitic propaganda within Thomas' speeches is incomparably greater than
the actual amount of his frank anti-Semitic statements. As we
pointed out, the medium by which he indirectly introduces
anti-Semitism is religion. This serves two purposes: to give
the attacks on the Jews an aura of theological authority and
to disguise his propaganda of hatred behind the cloak of
Christian love.
Palestine seems to function as a link between his theological
anti-Judaism and fascist anti-Semitism. This topic seems to be
fairly far-fetched. The resettlement of the Jews appears, at
first sight, to be of little emotional appeal to anti-Semites. Yet
the choice of this subject matter may not be altogether
insignificant. One of the fundamental impulses of the anti-
Semite makes itself felt in the complaint that the Jews are
"there." "They shall get out." "They are not wanted here."
While this impulse is apparently directed only against the
Jews as the "guest nation," a favorite Nazi concept, it actually
aims at the Jews being "there" at all. It is as though the anti-
Semite could not tolerate them on any part of the earth. He
regards them as intruders and infringers *everywhere*: in the
theatre, where they have bought their tickets as well as the
"Gentiles," no less than in the vacation resort or in an exotic
country. Their very existence is perceived by him as a threat
to the potentiality of feeling "at home." While he attacks the

Jews because of their supposed striving for world domination, the anti-Semite nourishes this desire himself. The Jews are a symbol to him that he does not yet possess the whole world. Hence the reference to Jewish settlement and Jewish expansion in a particular country probably has a definite meaning to the anti-Semitic-minded. It may inspire their fury even if the pertinent explicit statements. do not involve name-calling. This may help to understand why Thomas sometimes uses confused references to the Jewish resettlement of Palestine as symbols for the coming of the day of judgement, without making it quite clear whether he favors this settlement or resents it. This attitude mirrors the Nazi ambivalence toward Zionism. The Nazis welcomed it insofar as it promised that they could get rid of the Jews. But they also regarded it as dangerous – or at least pretended to so regard it – because it apparently proved their assumption of a Jewish nationalism transcending the borders of the other nations. Behind this ambivalence looms the most deadly hatred. The Jews, according to the fascist mentality, should be allowed neither to stay where they are nor to become a separate nation. No possibility is left but extermination. The Jewish settlement in Palestine is described in a factual manner, but its very phrasing has a threatening aspect. The audience is made to shudder under the idea of the supposedly tremendous increase of Jewish power in Palestine. The Jews are depicted as extremely formidable and, therefore, dangerous. We shall accompany the following passage by a running commentary.

Now, the Jews are returning. According to the Jewish telegraphic agency, recently, more Jewish farmers had been settled in Palestine than were there 2000 years ago. It is the one bright spot, economically speaking, in all the world today. There is no depression in Palestine. (The implication is, of course, that the Jews are smart and are doing well.) The natural resources of that nation (speaking about "that nation" is one of Thomas' standard devices. While this expression can apparently be explained on purely grammatical grounds, it psychologically conveys the idea of a nation that everyone knows but will not name) are now being exploited and developed. I was reading a report not long ago concerning the chemicals deposited in the Dead Sea (conspiratory device). This chemical research engineer said that somewhere between fifteen and twenty-five billion dollars

worth of vital chemicals were deposited in the Dead Sea alone.
(This is shrewdly ambiguous. It is left obscure whether Thomas refers
to the potential chemical value of the resources of the Dead Sea, or
whether he means that the Jews have hidden poisoned gas on its
ground, the intention being, that his uneducated listeners will
believe the latter. The idea, of course, is completely fantastic.)
On the Jordan river great hydro-electric plants are now being
developed. (Here a shock is achieved by the blasphemous combining
of a sacred Biblical name with a very modern technical term.)
Universities are springing up. My friend, this is a certain sign that
the hour of the Gentile nations is now closing. Why? Because the
Gentile nations are now doing exactly the same thing, yea, they have
already done so, that the Jews did 2000 years ago that caused their
Jewish expulsion from the land and caused God to reject the Jewish
nation. (The sins of the Gentiles are put upon the shoulders of the
Jews. The emphasis of the obscure sentence is upon the last words
"to reject the Jewish nation" and this is probably all the audience's
mind is capable of catching.) Now, then, they have been scattered,
and for 2000 years they have been a homeless and a wandering
people, wandering hither and yonder. In the meantime God has been
speaking and has given the authority to the Gentile nations. Now,
coincidentally with the close of the Gentile era the Jews are returning,
many of them to our Lord and Savior Jesus Christ. (This apparently positive sentence only contributes to the general confusion and
atmosphere of panic. Moreover, the implication is that baptized
Palestinian Jews may be saved and that the most degraded of all is
the Jew who remains where he is and clings to Judaism. This passage
hits ultimately at the Jews in America.) However, more of them are
returning to Palestine in unbelief. But, my friend, the hour is not far
away, when the armies yonder of the Gentile worlds in that great
battle of Armageddon, which will come in my opinion in the close of
the next great world war, the Jews shall be gathered in that land.
They shall be besieged upon every hand, and they shall fall upon
their faces, and in the hour of their extreme necessity, they will call
upon God and God will answer from Heaven; and Jesus Christ,
whom they have rejected, their elder brother, shall come with a
mighty delivering power.[16]

In other words, after the big pogrom that Thomas, the Nazi,
hopes for, Thomas the preacher gives them some chance of
being saved. Amazingly enough, the idea that a reckoning
with the Jews will take place after the second world war
appeared in Thomas' speeches eight years ago. This is one of
the major anti-Semitic slogans at present (1943). There is no

16 June 16, 1935.

doubt that this idea, dangerously spread among soldiers, was consciously manipulated by fascist agitators, and is quite independent of the war and the behaviour of Jews during the war. It has been warmed up artificially.

The main device of Thomas' indirect anti-Semitic propaganda is to refer to some Biblical guilt of the Jews. He depends upon his audience to transfer the age-old judgment to the present:

To the South was Isaiah, a contemporary of Hosea who was preaching in the South of Judea. Both men had practically the same message. God warned the nation through the lips of his prophet that unless the nation returned to God and established justice and mercy in the land, that inevitably God always allowed them to go down as a nation and to go into captivity and to be overrun by the surrounding nations of the world.[17]

Thomas goes on to compare present-day America to Judea at the time of the prophets. The major effect of the reiteration of the word Judea is to give the audience the idea that there exists a more immediate relationship between Judea and America, namely that the "American crisis" is due to the sons of Judea. Thomas is cautious not to make any such statement, but the "musical" setup of the whole passage with the drumming on "Jews" and "Judea" definitely works to that effect. This "musical" technique of anti-Semitic innuendo is most obvious in this statement: "Communism is nothing more or less than the synagogue of Satan that our Lord spoke about."[18] The description of Communism as the synagogue of Satan is superficially only a Biblical metaphor; but since Jewish temples are known under the Greek name of synagogue, the association carried by the sentence is that Communism has something to do with the synagogues – in other words, that Jews and Communists are the same.

"Problem" device

Sometimes Thomas comes into the open with frank anti-Semitic statements. Primary, of course, is insistence upon the "Jewish

17 June 2, 1935.
18 June 21, 1935.

problem" in America. In a democracy, anti-Semitism has won
its first victory when the farce of such a "problem" is allowed
to go on. It is a particularly easy and dangerous victory since
the term "problem" appears to be neutral and scientific. But
actually this term brings about a conceptual segregation of
the Jews and implies that they are going to become the
object of certain special administrative measures. The "problem" device requires a special technique of pseudo-objectivity.
In the very moment when Thomas becomes an outspoken
anti-Semite, he professes to be a friend of the Jews. This
highly significant configuration has the following appearance:

In every nation of the world today, you have that tremendous
conflict going on between the Jews with the government and the
people that are represented within that nation. There is not a nation
in the world today that does not have its Jewish problem, not one.
I speak, tonight (!), as a friend of the Jews. I speak, tonight, as one
that would take the Gospel of Jesus Christ to them, but I say to you
without any fear of contradiction: There is a Jewish problem on at
the present hour that will not die throughout the earth. It is the
precursor, it is the forerunner of that day, there, that hour when that
people shall be gathered yonder in that great land, going back in
unbelief; but one of these days they will cry to Jesus Christ to release
them and he shall come and claim his ancient people. ... Is it not a
fault of the Christians of the world that we have failed to take the
Gospel of Jesus Christ to that people? We are reaping what we have
sown, we are reaping what we have sown.[19]

The last sentence hypocritically blames the Christians who
have failed to convert the Jews, implying that the Jews are
going to punish them for this failure. In reality, behind the
gesture of repentance looms the Jewish danger and the Communist world plot, serving as an incitement to "defensive"
action. This is achieved by a Biblical quotation that follows
immediately after the last sentences: "They shall fall by the
edge of the sword, and Jerusalem shall be trodden until the
time of the Gentiles shall come."[20] In this context the application of the citation is quite clear. The Jews are supposed to
rule the world, until the Gentiles unite against them. Hardly
less clear is the idea promoted by the following statement,

19 June 13, 1935.
20 *Ibid.*

where confusion fosters panic and makes the issue against the Jews even stronger:

"... that Jerusalem is in the hand of the Jews again, that it is the national home reestablished for the Jews. The Jews are now in the land of Palestine in answer to the prophecy of God. There are more Jews there now than any time in 2000 years of history. (This is supposed to be a threat to the Gentiles.) In 1917 it was a critical time in the history of the earth of ours. Now, strange as it may seem, do you know that when General Allenby took the city of Jerusalem in the name of King George ... from the very moment God placed it in the hands of the Zionists, from that hour other things happened. The Communists moved into Moscow exactly upon the release of Palestine. The Church began a downward movement, a loss of vitality, a loss of life. What else happened? You find the program of the Antichrist moving across the world in order to fasten the hold upon the world through all Christian homes in this world of ours.[21]

The idea is that the Zionists, the British and the Communists were all involved in a huge conspiracy. This linking, by the way, corresponds to a line of attack taken by other fascist agitators, such as Phelps, who include the English in their Jew-baiting and Communist-baiting. In fact, the Nazi government called the British, "white Jews."

In general the identification of the Jews with the Devil (as Christ-killers) leads to an image of them as diabolical plotters throughout the history of the world. This line of attack is favored by Thomas above that of depicting them as emulators, characterless intruders, "Untermenschen," etc. Here lies a specific difference between German and American anti-Semitism. It should be taken into consideration by counterpropaganda. German Jews, most of whom had been native for many centuries, were largely assimilated. Anti-Semitism had to attack them in their assimilated condition. Hence, it exploited the concept of assimilation itself. Jews were depicted as aiming to merge with Gentiles – to "poison" them from within. In America, where Jewish immigration on a large scale took place only since the nineteenth century, assimilation is by no means so strongly developed, and the Jewish immigrants are a much more obvious national minority. Hence, the job of anti-Semi-

21 July 6, 1935.

tism is easier in a way. Jews are blamed for being different. This is expressed in the prevailing idea of American anti-Semitism that the Jews are conspirators and aim at political supremacy as a definite national group. It should be noted, however, that in Thomas' anti-Semitic armory at least one argument is utterly lacking – the idea of the Jew as a weakling. This argument probably proved to be the most dangerous of all in Germany. The Biblical splendour with which Thomas cloaks the Jews is, in spite of his antipathy, a kind of safe-guard against contempt and derision. It is this reason which made Thomas comparatively innocuous in his specific cam-paign against the Jews. It is perhaps correct to say that those of his techniques which have nothing to do with the Jews are psychologically more dangerous as anti-Semitic weapons than his anti-Semitic invectives themselves.

Remarks on Thomas' appeal to Americanism cannot be compared with the emphasis Nazi agitators put on their idea of the fatherland and the German race. Thomas' Americanism is only a somewhat feeble echo. His moderation is probably due to his adaption to the mood of his listeners. In foreign policy, he exploits pacifism in the same way as he exploits anticapitalist leanings in home policy. Militant patriotism is much less developed in a country which has undergone few foreign wars and whose predominance has remained undisput-ed. Hence Thomas' Americanism is of a somewhat negative nature. He speaks of the danger threatening this country and of its having become soft and decadent, much more than of its strength or its right to a dominant position in the world. His foreign policy consists of patriotic exaltation and a simultaneous resignation to the power aspirations of other countries. He favors nationalism as such. Concretely, however, he sympathizes more with German nationalism, the model for his fascist ideals, than with the foreign political aims of the American nation.

This is reflected by a certain ambivalence in regard to the problem of war, which of course plays the Nazi game. In spite of his Americanism – or rather because of his fascist concept for America – Thomas is an appeaser. He uses American peace-mindedness as a force for bringing the country into the clutches of the aggressor nations. He presents a long and confused argument which terminates in a kind of justification of German rearmament.

There is absolutely no comparison of what has taken place in the world as to what is going to take place in the world. Every states-man in the world is absolutely shivering in his boots for the fear of what is coming upon the morrow. The British statesmen, every one of them, say that war cannot be postponed in Europe so very much longer. France and Germany, and Italy, and England, and Russia, and every nation and Japan are ready. They are armed to the teeth. They are ready for the beginning of the Hell upon earth. Not that any one of the nations wants it. It is my opinion that every states-man in Europe despises war. If they know anything about it, they despise it. When anybody tells you that there is a lot of saber rattling going on in the world, men that want war, I don't believe that any sane man desires war, but in spite of the fact that they do not desire war, they are being pushed inevitably step by step, inch by inch over the abyss into another great world patricidal conflict. Why is it? Why is it that we can't stop war? Why is it that the Commu-nists in this country preach that America shall disarm, but allow Russia to arm? Now, I don't take any stock in that type of pacifism at all, and I don't think that any man or American that has his head upon his shoulders and eyes that see, that are wide open and a brain that is thinking, takes any stock in that type of thing, but listen, why is it that we can't stop war? For the very simple thing that this world lies in the lap of the wicked ones. For the very simple reason that this world has rejected the Son of the living God. The world system is not based upon Christianity. The world system is based upon a satanic world, that desires to devour and desires to kill and desires to murder the human race. Now, the nations of the world are getting prepared. Now, you mind what I tell you. I know, when war comes again, and it will come, you know the wars have been interspaced approximately twenty years between. ... The last war, it will only be a child's play as compared to the war that is coming. Can you imagine a hundred airplanes in the stratosphere, piloted by robots with great bombs sent out two miles high, where it is utterly impossible to make a defense so far as other planes are concerned, and with the proper setting of a watch to drop two great bombs two to three miles high in the midst of a great city in the world. Why, my friends, you know what it means. It means annihilation. It means death. It means destruction. Can you imagine what the next war will be? There will be machine guns firing six thousand shots a minute. Can you imagine that? Well, now listen to

me. Nobody that has any sense desires war, but there is something on
the inside of the human race that is producing fear. Germany fears.
That is the reason that Germany is arming.[22]

His foreign political line is definitely pro-German:

You will note a manoeuvering going on between Italy, France, and
England and that of Germany on the other side. I am happy to note
that apparently a new program is gradually being evolved between,
or by the British nation in their attitude toward the German people.
I think that it is now well conceded in high diplomatic circles that
the Germanic races, and the Anglo-Saxon races and the Scandinavian races must now all stand shoulder to shoulder against this greatest
menace that has ever faced Western civilization since Genghis Khan
launched his hordes of Asiatics and overran the Western world. England seems to be softening towards Germany, knowing full well that
Germany stands as the only bulwark of Western civilization against
the great hordes of Communists, under the leadership of the apostate
people, and that unless the Germanic and English speaking nations
stand together, there is no hope of preserving the Christian religion
or the Christian civilization. And if our own officials in Washington
are wise, they will chart a national course that will bring Great
Britain, Germany, and the Scandinavian nations into a fraternal
understanding.[23]

Whereas the "apostate people," whoever these may be, are
godless, the Nazis are regarded, by hook or crook, as being
religious:

God had to allow Germany to bleed to death until the German
people came to realize that there is God in Heaven and that the
nation that forgets God goes down to utter defeat. My friend, Germany today has learned her lesson, and has begun to come back and
realize that the religion must go out and word of God must be
praised. England and America will go down.[24]

Authoritarian obedience seemingly is regarded as being religious *per se*. Here the preaching of religious repentance moves
surreptitiously into the doctrines of a fifth columnist. It is
against this background that the "supreme demand of the
hour" is brought out.

It should be added that Thomas uses a peculiar technique
when he deals with foreign policy. Nations are treated by him

22 April 27, 1935.
23 April 14, 1935.
24 April 25, 1935.

as if they were subjects. Moral concepts are immediately applied to them and moral dichotomies are used to explain national political issues. This device, a concession to the incapacity of the audience to think in impersonal terms, has a sinister connotation in spite of its prophetic ring. The more the nations are treated as single subjects rather than as groups of people, and the more people are made obedient cogs within their nations, the more helplessly are they subject to the impending catastrophe which Thomas incessantly depicts. Thus they are being softened up for "integration."

The Bible makes plain to us, my friend, the reason for the fall of the empires. There is a moral law at work among the nations, for nations are but made up of men and women. Whatever a man soweth, that shall he reap. Whatever a nation soweth, that shall it also reap. Wide, indeed, is the field of observation when we come to study this truth of the past and the present, for nations are just as surely dying and sinking, today, as they have been in the past, for every monument and every book and arch and every heap of debris, every lonely pillar becomes a pulpit from which we hear the voice of the past, preaching the great sermon of national sin and national judgment.[25]

The personification of the nation is a kind of negative totalitarian integration. The American nation, according to Thomas, is a huge collective sinner; therefore, the nation has to repent collectively – in short, adopt a fascist order.

God is calling the American people to return to himself. He says, I have a controversy against you, because you have departed from me, from my covenant. You have broken my ordinance. You and I, my friend, are part and parcel of a great people. Our forefathers in this nation have built a great structure, and they planted this word of the living God as the very foundation stone of their individual life, of their state life, and of their national life, and now we have broken upon difficult days. We have come to days, my friend, when we have disregarded the old landmarks of our fathers. We have become so wise. We have become so understanding. We know everything but, ah, my friends, there are some things that we don't know, and that is we have lost a knowledge of the living God out of these lives of ours. America, today, is an unhappy land. America, today, is an unhappy people. From the Atlantic to the Pacific, from the Dominion of Canada to the Gulf of Mexico, our people are in a

25 July 14, 1935.

chaotic state of evils. My friend, the reason for that is simply this. We have kicked the knowledge of our God out of our hearts and minds. We are doing a lot of sacrificing, today, sacrificing to the wrong things. We sacrifice to the God of silver and gold. We bow down to hay and stubble. The God of the belly is our God, today upon the part of many of our people. The God of pleasure has taken the place of the God of obedience; our Lord, Jesus Christ has been cast out of our churches .... Our fathers wanted to get to a point where God could rule their lives and the lives of their children and so they came across the uncharted ocean, across these plains and prairies and mountains. They lived in sod houses. They lived in log houses. They lived in the dugouts beneath the earth.[26]

Characteristically enough, the appeal for American regeneration ends with an almost unveiled desire for a lowering of the general standard of living. This change which he expects to be brought about by totalitarian regimentation is rationalized as being God's remedy for softness and degeneration.

Conclusion

The ultimate aim of Thomas' propaganda is authority by brutal, sadistic oppression. This is the focal point, the unifying principle that rules his theology and his politics, his psychology and his morals. Among his stimuli the concept of severe punishment in time and eternity is decisive. His descriptions of tortures are minute in detail. Obviously he wants to give his listeners a special gratification through such descriptions.

They built a fire for him one day, and they said, Polycarp, unless you recant, unless you denounce Jesus Christ, then, indeed, you must burn. It is said that he reached his right hand into the flame and gave to the world this historical statement. "Three score and ten years have I served the Christ, and he has done me no harm but only good. Why should I renounce him now in my old age?" He refused to recant that Jesus Christ is the Son of God. Polycarp, when he had ended those words in substance, walked into the flames and was burned to a crisp, and it was during the same period of time when tens of thousands of Christians were cast into prison. We are told that tens of thousands of these men, women, and children were fed to the lions, that they marched proudly with their faces turned toward God

26 June 9, 1935.

into the bloodiest arena and there kneeling down, they committed their souls to the Christ; that the lions with a bound were upon them and crunched their bones and ate their flesh. We are told in this period of time, that the fires and the water and every conceivable form of persecution was used in order to do away with Christianity; but instead of the Christians decreasing, they increased. They were driven into the holes of the earth; – and today, we have found the remains of many of them beneath the catacombs ... hidden from the soldiers, hidden from the secret police ... hidden from the spying eyes, these men and women lived and died in a triumphant faith. I call your attention here to the fact that our Lord, Jesus Christ, said that those days of tribulation will come, be thou faithful until death, and I will give you the crown of life.[27]

The future of America of which he warns is depicted in not altogether different terms: "One of these fine mornings you men and women will arise with no stocks and no bonds and no home and your backs will be placed against a wall with a machine gun bullet in your heart and in your head."[28] One may well expect that the audience projects this image upon their foes and thus enjoys it. Thomas almost openly professes this ambivalence towards atrocities in one of his anti-Soviet diatribes: "I want to say that you men and women, you and I are living in the most fearful time of the history of the world. We are living also in the most gracious and most wonderful time."[29] This is the agitator's dream, the unification of the horrible and the wonderful, the drunkenness of an annihilation that pretends to be salvation.

27 June 21, 1935.
28 July 7, 1935.
29 April 21, 1935.

The authorized representative in the EU for product safety and compliance is:
Mare Nostrum Group
B.V Doelen 72
4831 GR Breda
The Netherlands

www.ingramcontent.com/pod-product-compliance
Lightning Source LLC
Chambersburg PA
CBHW030610270326
41927CB00007B/1113

* 9 7 8 0 8 0 4 7 4 0 0 3 6 *